INVEST WITH YOUR EYES
EYES
NOT YOUR EARS

Order this book online at www.trafford.com
or email orders@trafford.com

Most Trafford titles are also available at major online book retailers.

Printed in Victoria, BC, Canada.

ISBN: 978-1-4251-8823-8

*Our mission is to efficiently provide the world's finest, most comprehensive
book publishing service, enabling every author to experience success.
To find out how to publish your book, your way, and have it available
worldwide, visit us online at www.trafford.com*

Trafford rev. 2/22/10

www.trafford.com

North America & international
toll-free: 1 888 232 4444 (USA & Canada)
phone: 250 383 6864 ♦ fax: 812 355 4082

Dedication

To my wonderful wife Laurie, who supported and assisted me with the researching, writing and editing these past 11 years, and whose advice and guidance helped to see me through this major undertaking.

Your love and unwavering encouragement inspired me to compile and present these timeless truths in the hopes of assisting my fellow investors in their quest for greater returns.

Acknowledgments

I thank my mother Wanda for her love and guidance which contributes so much to the person that I am, allowing me to go forward in this life with the confidence not only to improve myself day by day, but also to help others as I travel along my path.

I thank my friends, Mr. W. Feather & Associates who whole-heartedly offered up their love and guidance, inspiring in me the enthusiasm and creativity to accomplish this life long goal.

And, thank you to Prophet Financial Systems (www.prophet.net) for the use of their charts.

"Expert: someone who brings confusion to simplicity."

- John Kendrick Bangs

Let be known that it is not the intent of this book to identify or single out who the Manipulators are. There have been no attempts to directly or indirectly name or imply the identity of any person or groups involved in the participation of manipulation. This book focuses rather on the obvious presence and significant involvement of manipulation in the financial markets, and how that involvement affects you as an investor.

Also, please be aware that there is significant risk associated with investing in the stock market (especially for those who approach investing using the so-called "tried and true" methods). With that said, the main focus of this book is to assist investors with an understanding that continued study and practice, coupled with a new kind of faith, will help to put the odds back in your favour.

Contents

Preface

The truth is often times right in front of our eyes and we don't even realize it. We see the world through our own perceptions and don't allow ourselves to open our minds – our **EYES**, to other possibilities.

The truth is simple, consistent, permanent and always present, but sometimes we push it under the surface in favour of more complicated explanations. The purpose of this book is to reveal to you what is right in front of your eyes. It will seem so obvious that you may want to discard it without much thought, but beware – that is exactly what THEY are counting on.

Don't fall into THEIR trap. This truth has been at the heart of every financial market for decades and will continue for decades to come. THEY prey upon your inability to control your emotions. Left unchecked, uncontrolled, you have little chance of success investing in the equity markets. Only awareness and practice will allow you to keep at bay that which is so natural to you. The most integral part of your psyche is being turned and used against you. That which makes you unique among all beings is being exploited. You must come to realize that this practice is commonplace and you must learn to shield yourself against its detrimental effects.

This book will reveal to you what THEY don't want you to know, their greatest secret – that which enables them to consistently profit at your expense. You will learn how they are able to accomplish this feat, as regular as clockwork, time and time again, year after year. You will learn how they go about leading the unsuspecting public astray. And most importantly, you will learn how to recognize their methods and how to employ those same techniques for your own financial success.

That is exactly what is available to you provided you read, re-read, realize, study and practice. Awareness and frequency grows confidence and greater confidence translates into greater control.

Introduction

<u>The Playing Field</u>

You must come to realize that all stocks are the same. The same in that they all move in a repeatable, predictable, orderly fashion. Well, how can this be? Are stocks not a fluid, spontaneous, ever changing set of variables, involving millions of people, trading billions of dollars every day all over the world? How could they all possibly act in the same manner, follow the same cycle.

The simple truth is - they do.

In order for them to follow this pattern, you will need to understand that if the markets are not happening by chance, as THEY would have you believe - then they must be controlled. That is after all, the only way they could share the same repeatable cycles, year after year, decade after decade.

I'm sure you're asking yourself, "If this is the case, then who is controlling them, and why, and how could they manage such a feat?" The markets involve millions of people trading billions of dollars daily, how could someone, anyone possibly control that?

In answer to those questions: in as far as "WHO", we'll get to that shortly. "WHY" is quite simply explained with a one word answer, "money". There are, unfortunately, very few things in life that motivate people as vigorously as money. Except for maybe love, money is at the top of the list of reasons why people are driven to do what they do. And, unfortunately, when money is involved, especially great sums of money - ethics, morals, and virtues give way to greed, selfishness and want. A good deal of this book will be dedicated to understanding the "HOW". If you can come to trust these cycles, then you will be well on your way to creating the kind of financial security that you desire.

Let's start with the **"MAN-MADE PRICE CYCLE"**. Remember all stocks move in this manner over and over again, and as long as man is involved, so too will these cycles repeat. If stocks, all stocks act this way, why can't I see it, recognize it, you ask? Because you have been conditioned to see things in a certain way. You are used to looking at stocks through a telephoto lens and, therefore, see only a magnified version of what is right in front of you. When you flip the telephoto setting back to normal view, all of a sudden your view enlarges and that which was previously hidden is revealed. And then, when you take yet another step back and remove the camera from in front of your eyes altogether, you take in the huge panorama that stands before you. It was always there, but because of the view setting you chose, you could not see all that was to be seen. The picture never changed, you just chose a narrow field of view and only focused on that which was but one chapter in a great volume of information.

This is what you must learn with regard to the stocks you intend to invest in. Step back and look at the big picture. See what has been in front of you all this time but which you haven't allowed yourself to see. By changing your field of view, you change the picture and your perspective. This is when, and only when the elusive price cycle will be revealed. Today's society is all about speed. Fast food, express lines, drive thru's, ATM's, it's everywhere. Unfortunately, it is easy to get caught up in this way of living and thinking and unconsciously transfer this same speedy approach to our investments. This is why we don't see what is right in front of us.

Step back and all will be revealed.

These cycles don't span hours, or days, or even weeks; they span months, years, and even decades. Long term price charts are your key to unlocking the treasure chest of information that has been previously buried. By long term, I mean charts that span 10 or 20 + years of price history. These are the charts that will not only give you the most accurate picture of what has happened in the past, but also valuable insight into what is about to happen in the future. Only by studying the long term price chart are you able to quickly identify which phase of the price cycle a stock is in, and hence whether it is a buy, a hold, a sell, or a "stay away". How else can you know if you are buying a stock in the lower price range unless you know what low really is? And, how can you know that unless you view the long term price history. Daily charts are a magnified view and are not a true indication of what is really happening.

You will come to understand why these cycles cannot occur more quickly and that if you attempt to shorten their natural workings, you will fall prey. It is THEY who create these man-made cycles – THEY who take advantage of your natural urge for speed.

There is no such thing as a quick easy buck but, unfortunately, the vast majority of us out there are trying to make it happen. Whether it is at the racetrack, the casino, in the lottery, or as a speculator in the markets, most people are convinced that they can somehow beat the odds and win. What they don't realize is that no one can defy the natural laws of the universe. They believe that they will somehow succeed where so many before them have failed. And, except for a very few, failure is the inevitable result.

The Law of Cause and Effect states that every effect in your life is the result of a specific cause, and if you trace back the cause and change it, you can change your result. Sow a seed and reap a harvest, sow a different seed and reap a different harvest.

Please understand that this is the #1 Law of the Universe and it applies to all aspects of your life, not just your investments. If you are not getting the results you desire in your work, your relationships, your education, or your health, then trace back the causes that are leading to those less than ideal situations (results in your life) and change them. It is the only way to get different results.

So then why do so many people attempt to bypass this truth? Every day hundreds, thousands, millions of people attempt to get different results in their lives from participating in the same causes that led to failure for themselves and the multitudes before them.

Is it not obvious that in order to get a different result in your life (reap a different success harvest), you must sow different seeds (engage in actions that have led to success for others). You don't plant pumpkin seeds and expect to grow carrots. Then why do so many try to invest in the stock market using the same old ("tried and true methods") and expect to reap financial gain when not only they themselves, but so many before them have garnered less than positive results.

Well, then what's the answer? The answer is to sow the same seeds as those whose harvest is similar to that which you wish to reap. Or more simply, do what successful investors do to get the same successful results they get. Who is successful, who's getting the results? The MANIPULATORS, that's who.

> The dictionary defines Manipulation in this way:
> ### - to manage by unfair use of influence

That is exactly what they do. They manage the price activity in such a way as to unfairly influence you into making wrong decisions. The stock price cycle represents a certain psychology, a certain way of thinking – for the investing public that is. The long term price chart is your tool to reveal these workings. Remember when we took the camera from our eyes, and revealed the panorama that stood before us – the total picture. Well, the long term price chart gives us that complete picture and allows us to see the man-made price cycle for the first time.

The Man-Made Price Cycle

The **price cycle** is made up of four phases:

1. Accumulation
2. Markup
3. Distribution
4. Markdown

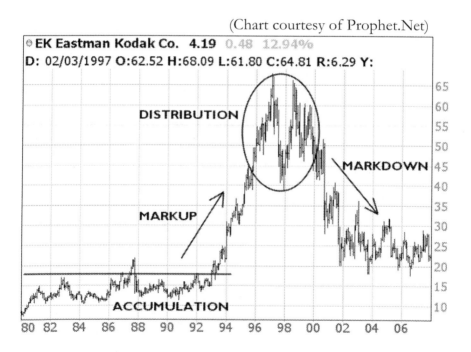

(Chart courtesy of Prophet.Net)

Accumulation is characterized by quiet, sideways price action in the bottom range. The markup phase is the period when prices are slowly rising off the bottom and making their way to new highs. Distribution is the violent price action that we see at the top of the rally and markdown is characterized by falling prices after distribution. When one price cycle ends another begins, and so on, and so on...

The Price Cycle could be likened to that of an expedition setting out to climb Mount Everest. During the early stages of the expedition, the team leader is securing a sponsor, choosing his team for their experience and skill, planning the route, acquiring the needed supplies, and checking weather forecasts, etc. Intensive planning goes into the climb but as of yet the team is still at ground level. This is very much like the **accumulation phase** of a stock, which is a representation of all the effort that is needed in advance of a rise.

(Chart courtesy of Prophet.Net)

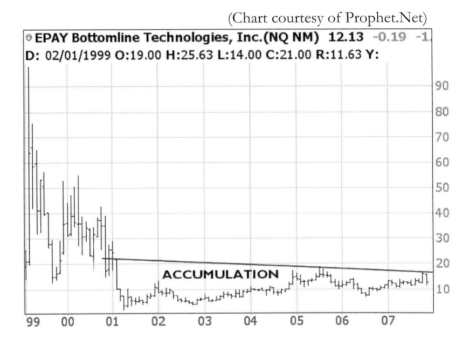

The team then slowly makes their way from the base of the mountain to base camp 1, and then to base camp 2, and then to base camp 3. Stopping from time to time to rest, refresh their supplies, and plan their route, the team experiences delays and setbacks along the way due to weather, altitude sickness, and fatigue. They are now making some steady headway towards their ultimate goal - the summit. This is very similar to the **markup phase** of a stock - slow consistent progress upwards from the base with setbacks and rest periods along the way.

A setback is defined as a temporary reversal in price.

(Chart courtesy of Prophet.Net)

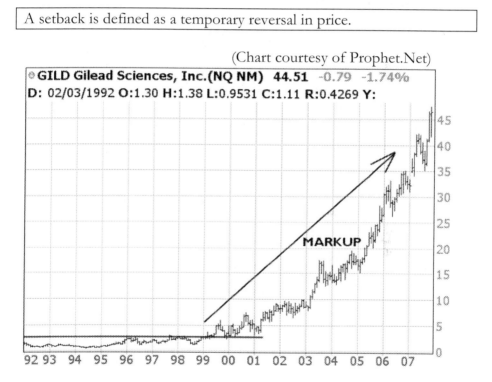

From base camp 3, the climbers execute their final assault on the peak. From here, members of the team make quick, upward thrusts toward the summit, each team attempting to reach the top and then descend just as quickly. This is exactly what happens during **distribution -** fast rising, volatile, up and down price action in the top range.

(Chart courtesy of Prophet.Net)

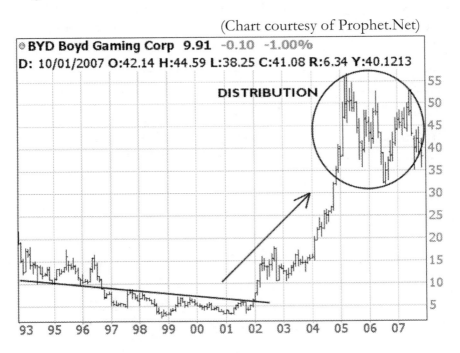

Once the team has reached their goal, they want to get back down the mountain as quickly as possible to avoid being caught in any potentially dangerous storms that are commonplace at the peak of Everest. Very much like the **markdown phase** of a stock, after reaching their peak, prices tend to tumble all the way back down to the base where they started their climb.

(Chart courtesy of Prophet.Net)

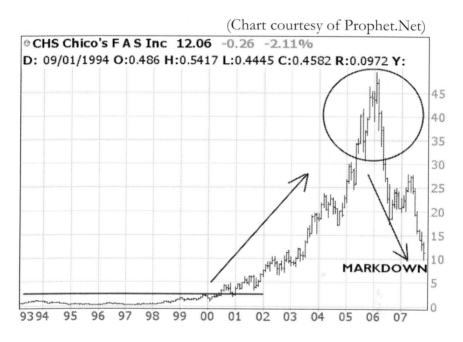

Be sure that all price mountains have different shapes and sizes just as real mountains are unique, but the overall cycle remains the same for all.

If you had made it to the top of Everest in the past and wanted to attempt another successful summit, you wouldn't likely change much about your preparation, your team, your route or you're planning, would you? The actions you took in your first summit attempt led to success and, therefore, will likely produce the same result the next time. Prices also follow the same pattern over and over. Why? Because what has worked in the past will work again in the future. The price cycle provides the Manipulators with their very best opportunity for success.

Please know that every stock, every commodity, acts in this manner. Regardless of what is happening around them, each individual stock follows its own price cycle, in its own time. This is where the big distinction takes place and this is why so many investors are led astray in their thinking.

If I were to ask you to characterize the money making opportunities in the stock market during 1998 and 1999 you would probably say "fantastic". The BULL market was raging, it seemed like everything was going up. You could have thrown a dart at the stock page and made money.

If I were to then ask you the same question about 2000 - 2003, you would probably say "terrible". Everything was falling, the BEAR had taken over and all those profits that you had made the previous years quickly evaporated. And in a lot of cases investors ended up worse off than when they started in 1998 or 1999.

Well, the simple fact of the matter is that the years 1998, 1999, 2000, 2001, 2002, and 2003 all offered up the <u>exact same</u> money making opportunities.

STOCK MARKET MYTH #1
<u>Bull versus Bear</u>

It's not about trying to decide whether we're in a Bull market or a Bear market. The secret lies in the fact that there is NO such thing as a Bull market or a Bear market to begin with. There are quite simply, accumulations, markups, distributions and markdowns of individual stocks. Be very clear about this.

There is no such thing as a BEAR or a BULL market.

Why do so many people put so much emphasis on "THE MARKET", "THE DOW", "THE NASDAQ"? They talk about them with an almost reverence, as if they are the "be all, end all" indicators of their success. Apparently if the DOW and NASDAQ are falling for a significant period of time, the experts and media will tell you that we are locked in a BEAR market and you will have a very hard time making positive returns until the market turns around. All I can say to that is hogwash.

Unless you invest in index funds,* you don't trade averages, so why would you take your direction from them, (* A passively managed fund that tries to mirror the performance of a specific index.). The DOW and the NASDAQ, as well as the TSX and the S&P 500 are merely an average rating of how 30, 100, 300 or 500 of the big cap, big name stocks are doing in their respective indices.

That doesn't mean that the other thousands of stocks being traded every day on those same exchanges are acting in favour with them. Now yes, the performance of these big cap, big names stocks do give us an indication about how the economy is doing overall. However, with that said, you as an individual are not bound by these averages, you are not bound by how the rest of the economy is doing, you are not bound by dire news from the media or the negative earnings reports from the country's largest companies. You are only bound by your awareness and your perceptions - your awareness of market Manipulation and your perceptions about time. Many stocks were making significant gains from 2000 - 2003 while the media darlings, (i.e., Microsoft, Sun Microsystems, Time Warner, IBM, Oracle, Nortel, et al) were all heading for the basement.

If you lost money during this period, it's not because of a BEAR market, it's because you were invested in stocks that were in markdown rather than stocks that were in markup – it's as simple as that.

Individual stocks go through their man-made price cycle in their own time which means that at any point in time, you will be able to find stocks that are rising (markup phase), stocks that are falling (markdown phase), stocks that are volatile (distribution) and stocks that are going sideways (accumulation). It's up to you to identify them and then choose appropriately. This is what we are going to examine throughout the course of this book. This new awareness will open you up to a whole new (very profitable) perspective.

(Chart courtesy of Prophet.Net)

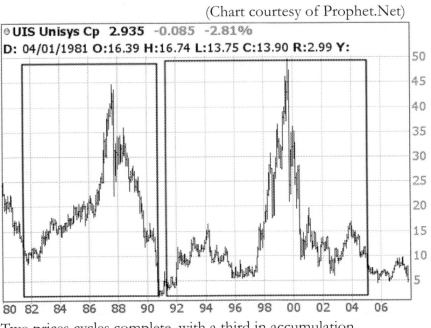

Two prices cycles complete, with a third in accumulation.

(Chart courtesy of Prophet.Net)

One price cycle complete with a second in markdown.

(Chart courtesy of Prophet.Net)

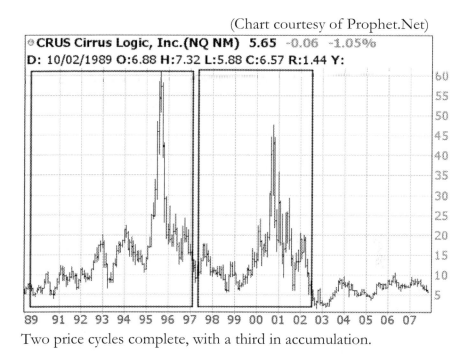

Two price cycles complete, with a third in accumulation.

(Chart courtesy of Prophet.Net)

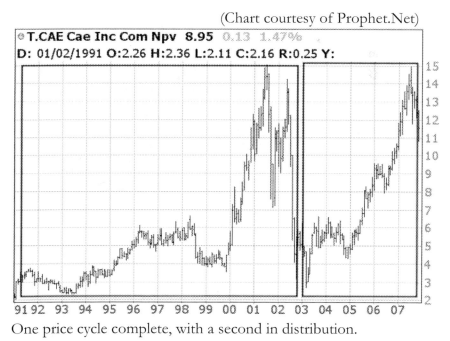

One price cycle complete, with a second in distribution.

Throughout the book I'll highlight (using a shaded box) what THEY refer to as a BEAR market - that time frame between 2000 and 2003. It is a reminder that we, as individual investors, are not bound by the perceptions of others. Regardless of what the media, experts and analysts all say, there is no such thing as a BEAR market as it relates to your individual opportunities.

Look at how UNH, defied "THE MARKET" as its markup phase started its climb at the exact same time as the S&P, the DOW and the NASDAQ (next two pages) all started their three year tumble.

(Chart courtesy of Prophet.Net)

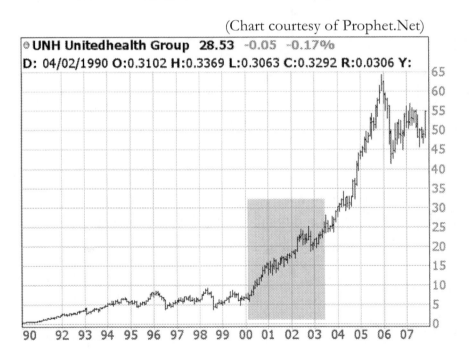

(Chart courtesy of Prophet.Net)

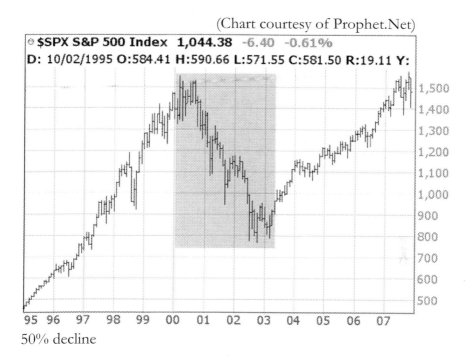

50% decline

(Chart courtesy of Prophet.Net)

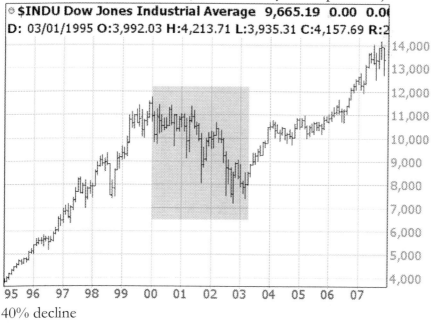

40% decline

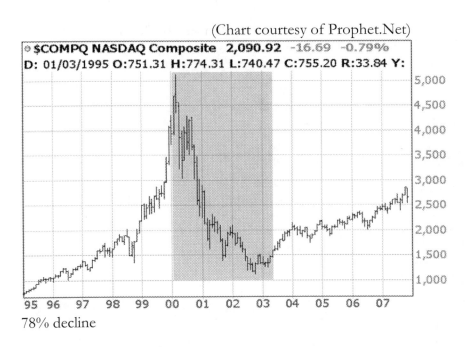

78% decline

Bear market and bull markets don't matter - accumulation and markup matter. While most of the investing public was riding big losses into even bigger losses from 2000 to 2003, UNH moved from $7.00 to $25.00 per share, a 257% rise.

And it wasn't alone.

Ball Corp. moved from $5.50 to $27.50 per share during this time (a 400% rise). Not something you'd expect if you were taking your cues from the S&P, the DOW or the NADSAQ.

(Chart courtesy of Prophet.Net)

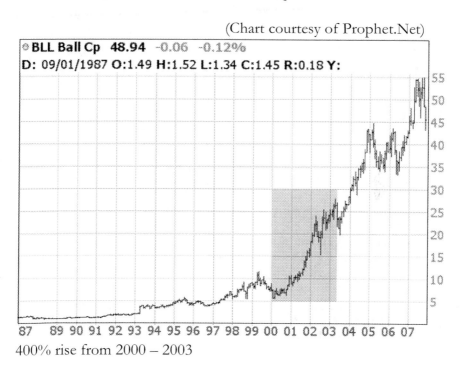

400% rise from 2000 – 2003

14

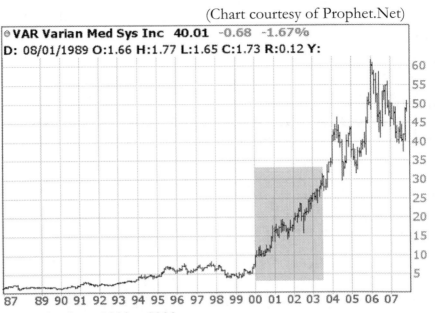

(Chart courtesy of Prophet.Net)

500% rise from 2000 – 2003

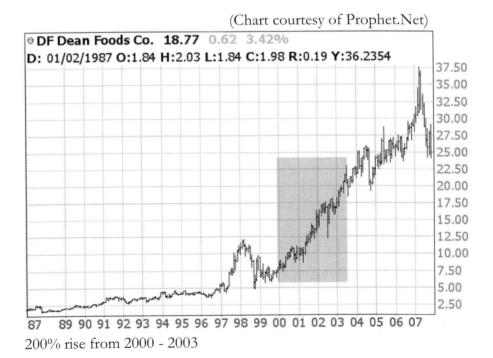

(Chart courtesy of Prophet.Net)

200% rise from 2000 - 2003

(Chart courtesy of Prophet.Net)

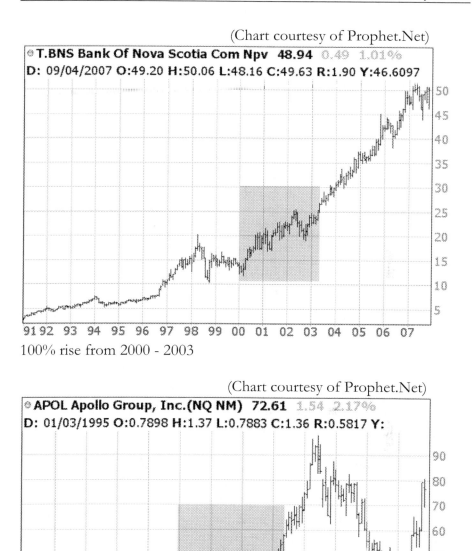

100% rise from 2000 - 2003

(Chart courtesy of Prophet.Net)

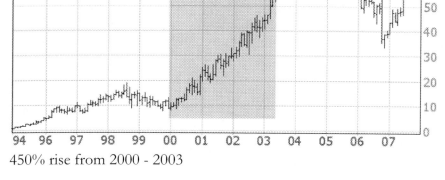

450% rise from 2000 - 2003

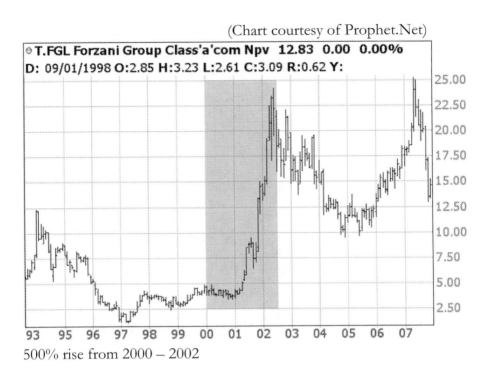

T.FGL Forzani Group Class'a'com Npv 12.83 0.00 0.00%
D: 09/01/1998 O:2.85 H:3.23 L:2.61 C:3.09 R:0.62 Y:

500% rise from 2000 – 2002

Well accumulated stocks don't care what the NASDAQ, the DOW, the TSX and the S&P are doing, they move based on their own manipulated price cycle.

The Manipulators are the ones who are controlling prices, not the speculators, the experts, analysts, or media. Nor is it the big name, big cap stocks which make up the composite indices and whose performance end up dictating what happens to the "magical" DOW and NASDAQ numbers each day. Just because all the widely-helds are on their way from the penthouse to the basement doesn't mean that UNH and other well accumulated stocks are going to follow suit. Their foundations are set in concrete and steel and the only ride for them is up.

(Chart courtesy of Prophet.Net)

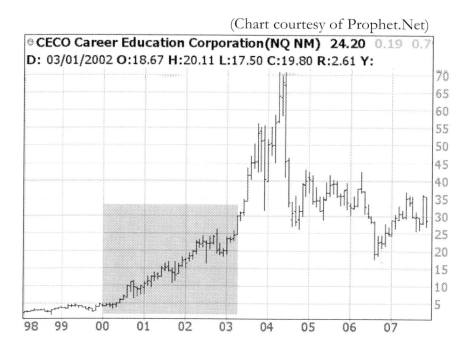

Career Education's shares rose from $5.00 to $30 between 2000 and 2003.   That's a 500% increase in value during their so-called "Bear" market.

What makes UNH, BLL, VAR, DF, T.BNS, APOL, T.FGL, and CECO different from the rest? Nothing. They were simply at that stage in their price cycle when they were moving from accumulation to markup whereas most of the big name, widely held stocks like Time Warner, IBM, Intel, and Microsoft, etc... were all moving from distribution to markdown.

Let's compare Western Digital, Cisco Systems, and Toll Brothers (next page). During the 90's and through to 2007, they all went through the same manipulated price cycle: an accumulation phase, a markup, a distribution phase and a markdown – just at different times. That is the only difference between them, <u>and all stocks</u> – the "WHEN" of each phase.

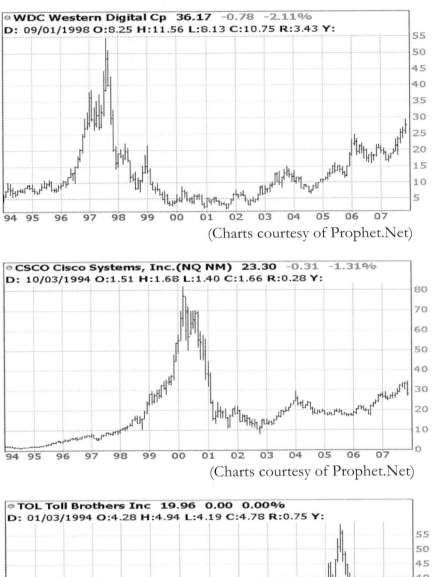

WDC Western Digital Cp   36.17   -0.78   -2.11%
D: 09/01/1998 O:8.25 H:11.56 L:8.13 C:10.75 R:3.43 Y:

(Charts courtesy of Prophet.Net)

CSCO Cisco Systems, Inc.(NQ NM)   23.30   -0.31   -1.31%
D: 10/03/1994 O:1.51 H:1.68 L:1.40 C:1.66 R:0.28 Y:

(Charts courtesy of Prophet.Net)

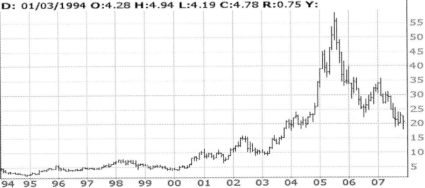

TOL Toll Brothers Inc   19.96   0.00   0.00%
D: 01/03/1994 O:4.28 H:4.94 L:4.19 C:4.78 R:0.75 Y:

ACCUMULATION➜MARKUP➜DISTRIBUTION➜MARK-DOWN➜ACCUMULATION...

The common denominator is the <u>manipulated price cycle</u>, not a BULL market or a BEAR market.

Every stock's price cycle will take a different shape and size, but they will be similar, and the reasoning behind each will always be the same - to **"discourage"** you out at the bottom and to **"excite"** you in at the top. How else can the Manipulators make money other than to buy low and sell high, and since there is always someone on the other side of every share that is traded, that leaves you and the rest of the investing public to bear the burden of **buying high** and **selling low**. Markups following long accumulations lead to significant moves. In the example of Western Digital, Cisco and Toll Brothers, up to 450%, 720% and 1100%, respectively.

We will come back to this discussion again a little later but for now, forget about BULL and BEAR and think in terms of accumulation, markup, distribution and markdown. And, just think about <u>one</u> stock at a time versus the entire market as a whole. You will come to recognize that these price cycles **PEAK** at their own time, and are not dependent on what the rest of the market is doing (as further evidenced by the following charts).

(Chart courtesy of Prophet.Net)

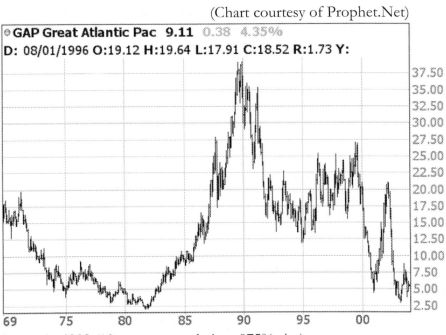

Summit: 1989 (10 year accumulation: 875% rise)

(Chart courtesy of Prophet.Net)

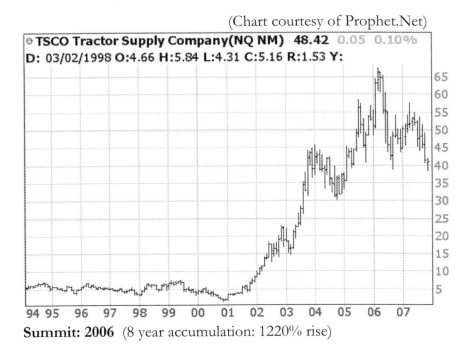

Summit: 2006 (8 year accumulation: 1220% rise)

(Chart courtesy of Prophet.Net)

Summit: 1998 9 year accumulation (not all shown) 450% rise

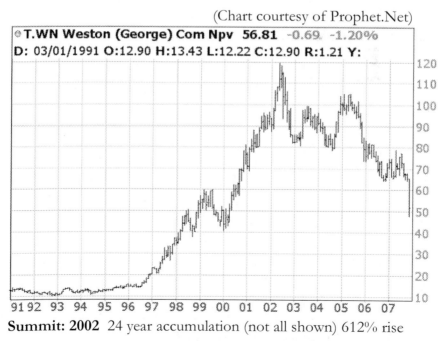

(Chart courtesy of Prophet.Net)

Summit: 2002 24 year accumulation (not all shown) 612% rise

(Chart courtesy of Prophet.Net)

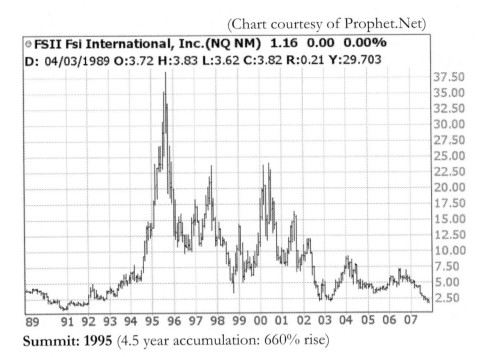

Summit: 1995 (4.5 year accumulation: 660% rise)

(Chart courtesy of Prophet.Net)

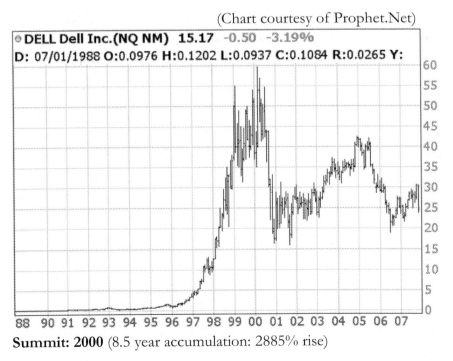

Summit: 2000 (8.5 year accumulation: 2885% rise)

(Chart courtesy of Prophet.Net)

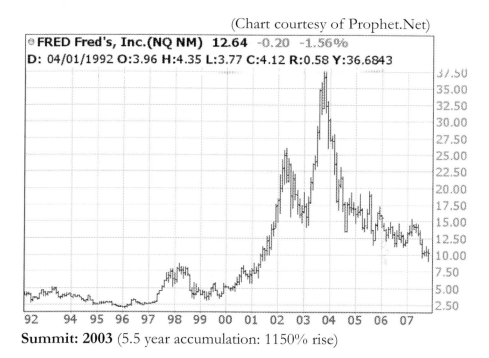

Summit: 2003 (5.5 year accumulation: 1150% rise)

(Chart courtesy of Prophet.Net)

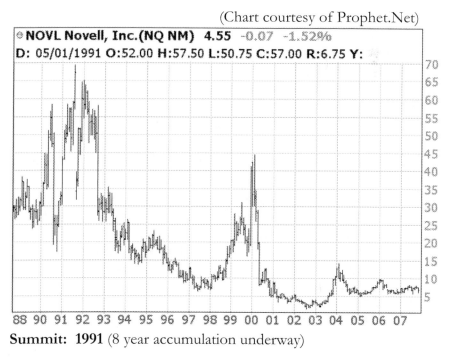

Summit: 1991 (8 year accumulation underway)

(Chart courtesy of Prophet.Net)

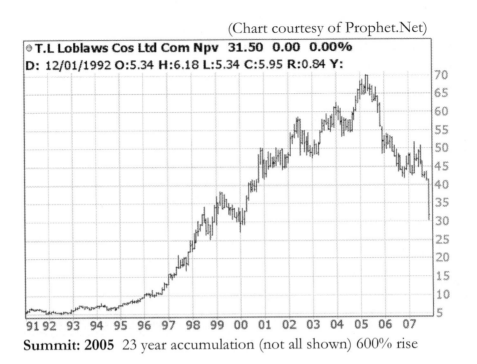

T.L Loblaws Cos Ltd Com Npv 31.50 0.00 0.00%
D: 12/01/1992 O:5.34 H:6.18 L:5.34 C:5.95 R:0.84 Y:

Summit: 2005 23 year accumulation (not all shown) 600% rise

(Chart courtesy of Prophet.Net)

BIG Big Lots Inc 24.43 0.31 1.29%
D: 10/03/1988 O:4.00 H:4.48 L:3.84 C:4.00 R:0.64 Y:

Summit: 1997 (6.5 year accumulation: 900% rise)

(Chart courtesy of Prophet.Net)

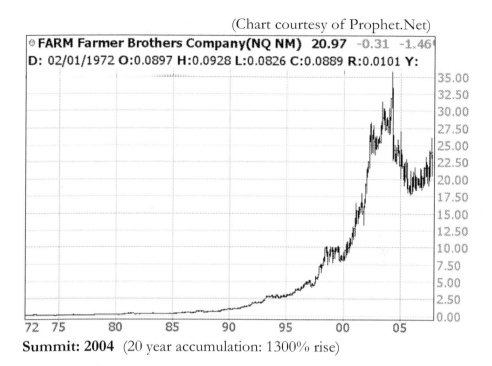

Summit: 2004 (20 year accumulation: 1300% rise)

Bull and Bear don't matter, ACCUMULATION and MARKUP matter.

The **WHEN** of each phase is the only difference between these stocks – all stocks.

Accumulation

It all begins and ends with accumulation. What does that mean? Very simply, this is when the Manipulators are buying. It seems natural doesn't it? Everybody knows to buy low and sell high. Well, if we all know, how come so many of us lost so much money, especially from 2000 – 2003. Was not the exact opposite the case? Did not millions of people buy high and sell low? That's the only way to lose money and we know the investing public lost billions of dollars so it must be true. The majority of people must buy high and sell low.

What keeps the public from buying down at the bottom, but eagerly willing to jump in at the top? Manipulation - that's what. Remember how we defined it earlier - managing by unfair use of influence. And, what do they manage unfairly – price action. They manage prices so as to make them appear discouraging to the public. Discouraging action is the reason we don't buy at the bottom.

The Manipulator's #1 weapon is discouraging action. Couple that with time (years and years of waiting for the next big move) and they have an unbeatable combination. What do WE all want, WE, meaning the investing public? We want encouraging price action = profits, and we want them fast. But, accumulation is just the opposite, it is discouraging and slow. That's why it's so easy for the public to justify that it is a good decision to sell if they are already in, or a good decision to stay out if they are on the sidelines watching.

What is discouraging action? The dictionary defines it as: **"deprived of courage, confidence and energy."**

That makes sense, if you don't have confidence in something; you're certainly not going to get involved whether it is a business deal, a relationship, or even a bet on your favourite football team.

Accumulation from the Manipulators' standpoint is just that, a price display lacking energy and confidence. Prices drift sideways with very little volume. They try to rally but each time they do, they hit an invisible barrier and fall back, sometimes to new lows. This is the discouraging type of action that keeps the public selling and the Manipulators buying. They are only too happy to scoop up all that they can in the bottom range. The public on the other hand is either ignoring it, or if they are already in - losing faith and selling.

(Chart courtesy of Prophet.Net)

CRDN Ceradyne, Inc.(NQ NM) 19.08 -0.01 -0.05%
D: 04/01/1985 O:5.17 H:5.23 L:4.85 C:4.95 R:0.38 Y:

19 year accumulation: 1580% rise

For Ceradyne, it seemed like a good idea to buy low, but when it wouldn't go up, and then went even lower, your only choice was to sell – that's what you thought anyway. You ran out of patience. If you were able to get out on a small rally you felt fortunate to have turned a profit and were only too happy to get out and move onto something else showing more promise. If you bought low and then sold lower, you were getting out for fear of bigger losses. You may have grown to hate what you once fell in love with, and then vow to never get back into that stock again. And, it's that kind of thinking that could turn out to be a big mistake.

Had you bought Ceradyne during the late 90's or even the early 2000's, would you have had the patience and confidence to hang in there while prices seemed to helplessly drift lower and lower? Probably not. If you had, you would have been rewarded very handsomely as prices rose upwards of 1600%. A little later we'll discuss optimizing your entry points so as to put the majority of the accumulation phase behind you, which will inevitably put you that much closer to the beginning of markup and profits. We'll also discuss how to hang on through the ups and downs of early markup to maximize your returns.

This price movement is not happening by chance. The Manipulators are moving price action in a discouraging manner (in this example from 1984 – 2003) for two reasons.

a) To keep you out, if you are not yet in AND,
b) to get you out, if you are already in.

How else would they be able to accumulate millions of shares in the bottom range over time, if these two criteria were not met? If large numbers of the public were buying as soon as prices hit bottom, then prices would immediately begin to rebound higher. More and more people would see the movement and buy because that is how they base a worthy investment, something that is already moving. This interest and volume would continue to attract more and more public buyers and the price of the stock would only spend a very short period of time in the bottom range. In turn, the Manipulators would then not be able to accumulate a large holding for themselves.

Earlier we talked about why the price cycle takes so long - as long as 3, 5, 8 years or, in some cases, as much as 20 years or more. If the Manipulators are controlling it, why don't they speed up the process and take their profits faster? Because they wouldn't be able to get the majority of the public out of the market, and hence wouldn't be able to accumulate a large enough holding for themselves. Taking more time during accumulation, worries more of the public out of the market, which in turn translates into more shares for the Manipulators at the bottom. This allows for more control during markup, which equates to more profits during distribution.

(Chart courtesy of Prophet.Net)

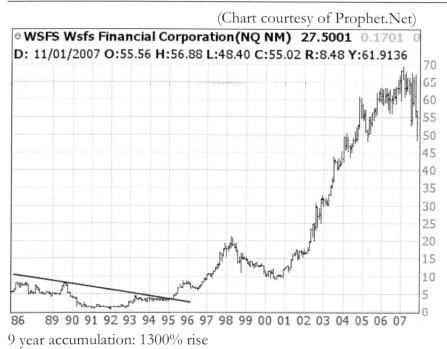

WSFS Wsfs Financial Corporation(NQ NM) 27.5001 0.1701 0
D: 11/01/2007 O:55.56 H:56.88 L:48.40 C:55.02 R:8.48 Y:61.9136

9 year accumulation: 1300% rise

For 9.5 years the Manipulators kept the price action down and discouraging on WSFS Financial until enough of the public lost faith and sold. (As you probably know, there is a limited number of shares in circulation for each stock so, when you want to sell your shares there has to be someone else on the other side of the transaction willing to buy them from you at that price. And conversely, when you want to purchase some stock, there has to be someone else on the other side of the transaction willing to sell it to you at that price).

So, as the public sold their shares of WSFS Financial over time, the Manipulators were standing by all the while ready and eager to buy them up as they were offered for sale. And, when the majority of the public was out, that is when, and only when, they decided to mark prices to higher levels.

Yes, it may take longer for the Manipulators to realize their profits but they have the resources and the patience to wait it out, something most investors will never have. By stretching out their purchases over time, they are able to keep prices down and buy up all the shares they desire in the bottom range.

They cannot buy in large quantities in a short period of time because they would defeat their own purpose. If the Manipulators bought too much too soon, prices would begin to move upwards and the public would become encouraged. And then, rather than selling to the Manipulators down at the bottom, the public's sentiment would grow more positive and they would at least be holding their shares if not buying more on the way up. This would in turn continue to drive prices higher and higher. The Manipulators would then have to stop buying and look for an opportunity to sell. They would have only accumulated a very small percentage of the total number of shares that they had originally intended to buy and, they would be selling them at prices much lower than they had originally targeted.

However, by the use of discouraging action, they can keep prices down in the bottom range and slowly accumulate as many shares as they require. A little later we will talk about exactly how they manage to keep prices down, and how they are able to maintain a discouraging attitude towards a stock for such a long period of time. But for now, just understand that this is why they do it.

Also, keep in mind that they have the resources to back up their plan. Some investors require the use of their money on a weekly or monthly basis to sustain their lifestyle. They need to draw on their reserves on a regular basis to sustain themselves. As well, many are trading with borrowed dollars and are making interest payments on that borrowed money. On the other hand, the Manipulators have huge cash reserves. They are quite capable of allotting millions of dollars towards an investment without gaining any return for years while not infringing on their lifestyle one little bit. This the kind of discipline and patience that you must learn to develop - the discipline not to invest more than you can comfortably do without, and the patience to wait for them to do what they must.

As the Manipulators control a larger and larger percentage of the outstanding shares of a stock (outstanding shares being defined as a limited number of common shares that are issued by a company and held by its investors), they gain more and more control, and the BASE (the support foundation where a rally begins), becomes stronger and stronger. This is our signal.

(Chart courtesy of Prophet.Net)

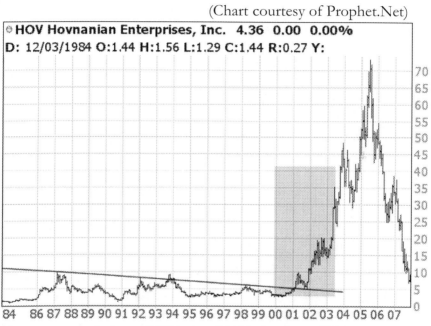

HOV Hovnanian Enterprises, Inc. 4.36 0.00 0.00%
D: 12/03/1984 O:1.44 H:1.56 L:1.29 C:1.44 R:0.27 Y:

18 year accumulation: 1360% rise (500% rise from 2000 – 2003)

- the greater the percentage of the public that is sold out, the stronger the base
- the longer the base, the stronger the base
- the stronger the base, the larger the rise

Accumulation is very similar to that of a political party holding a majority. As you know, when a party who forms the government holds a decided majority, they wield greater control because they have an easier time passing new legislation as all those who are voting, are members of the same family, "so to speak". They all have a common goal. The greater the majority, the easier it is for them to pass legislation and control policy.

On the flip side, if members of a different party held the majority, the first group would have a very hard time passing their legislation because they would have far fewer members voting in their favour. Hence, they would have little control as to the outcome of policy making.

So, for any party forming the government, it only makes sense that they would like to hold as large a majority as possible because with that comes more control and greater influence over outcomes.

This is exactly what is happening during the accumulation phase of a stock. The greater the number of shares held by the Manipulators, the greater control they have over price movement. This is the reason they want to shake the public out at the bottom.

This allows them to accumulate a large holding for themselves in the bottom range, and as they do it, they continually gain more and more control over the stock as they gain a larger and larger percentage of the outstanding shares available.

Hence, when they are ready to mark prices up to higher levels, they are able to accomplish this very easily because the public, on whole, would never be able to make enough shares available for sale (at any one time), to slow its progress.

The Base

What is a base? I think the easiest way to describe it would be to liken it to the foundation of a building. To quote Ted Warren from his book, "How To Make The Stock Market Make Money For You."

"Anyone building a temporary shack in the woods would not put much effort into building a really solid foundation under it. But if a person were to observe a deep excavation in which an extremely solid foundation was being poured, he would know that a high rise building was being built. An expert architect could even make a fair estimate as to how many stories it might be. Anyone would know that this extensive foundation was not being built for a mere shack. But few people realize that a quiet base of many years is the foundation for a "high rise", not a mere rally."

If the Manipulators don't spend much time using discouraging action to their benefit to accumulate a large holding, then you can be certain that, in most cases, a large rise will not follow. If, on the other hand, the long term price chart reveals to you a long quiet base of many years, you can be certain that a high rise is about to be built. The Manipulators have invested a lot of time and effort and money into building this foundation and their effort is revealed to you by a long period of quiet, discouraging price action.

(Chart courtesy of Prophet.Net)

10 year accumulation: 1625% rise (240% rise from 2000 – 2003)

A quiet base is just that, a picture of the time and effort that the Manipulators have invested. Whereas accumulation is the art of buying up millions of shares in the bottom range, the base itself is the formation that takes shape as a result of that buying. And, if their #1 goal is to profit, which of course it is, then doesn't it follow that the more time they spend, the more money they spend – the more they expect in return. It's only natural. It happens all around us every day.

For instance, if you were to help out on a project at work but only put in a few hours, you probably wouldn't expect much in the way of a reward, bonus or recognition. However, if you were to help out on another project where you invested months of effort, spent some of your weekends and evenings coming up with new ideas and, even contributed some of your personal money to the project, I'll bet when all was said and done – you would expect to be reimbursed for your expenses, rewarded significantly for your effort, and recognized publicly among your peers. As well you should – you invested a lot in that project. Well, the same is true for the Manipulators. The more time and effort and money that they invest, the more they expect in return. There's an old saying that sums it up nicely:

"THE MORE IN – THE MORE OUT"

Fortunately for us, the picture that results on the long term price chart is a direct representation of their investment - their effort. This is what we refer to as an accumulation base.

(Chart courtesy of Prophet.Net)

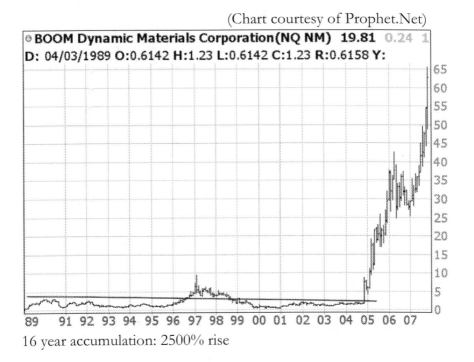

16 year accumulation: 2500% rise

Notice how the price action for BOOM (previous page) was very quiet during THEIR so-called 2000 – 2003 Bear market. On one hand, prices didn't rise during this period, however, on the other hand, they also didn't fall 40% or more as all the major North American indices did. Why? Because BOOM doesn't care about what the NASDAQ is doing. At that time, it was involved in its own accumulation phase, which is characterized by quiet, discouraging action. It acted true to form based on how it was being controlled as an individual stock rather than reacting to what was going on around it.

Have you ever seen a long term chart like this one and noticed the big rallies that have taken place. Most of us have. We think to ourselves, boy, I wish I had gotten a piece of that move. Have you ever asked yourself why you didn't? What caused you to miss yet another big move? Is it just chance that you seem to always miss the really big moves? Of course not. Your answer is right there on the long term price chart (but since you have been conditioned to view stocks with a telephoto lens – you never see it). Have you ever looked at the price action preceding these big moves? If you look at enough of them you will see a remarkable pattern. Almost every big rise is preceded by a long, quiet accumulation base - a period of extremely discouraging action. That is why you miss out.

BOOM traded under $3.00 for the better part of 14 years. And it was this long period of basing action which resulted in a 2500% rise. We'll talk a little later about buying and selling but for now, just become used to the idea that a quiet base of many years is the **foundation for a high rise, not a mere rally.**

(Chart courtesy of Prophet.Net)

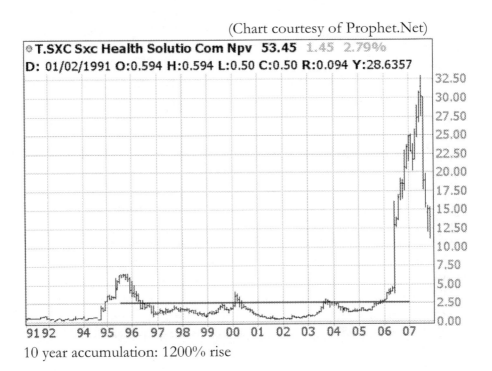

T.SXC Sxc Health Solutio Com Npv 53.45 1.45 2.79%
D: 01/02/1991 O:0.594 H:0.594 L:0.50 C:0.50 R:0.094 Y:28.6357

10 year accumulation: 1200% rise

We have to ask ourselves, and keep asking ourselves, what is the purpose of accumulation? Well, we have already talked about that, to enable the Manipulators to buy up huge quantities in the lower price range. But that's just part of the answer. Remember when we talked about the Manipulator's goals in the lower price range:

1. To keep you out, if you are not yet in AND,
2. to get you out, if you are already in.

These objectives serve two purposes. Yes, it allows them to accumulate at the bottom but secondly and just as important, it provides them with <u>someone to sell to at the top</u>. Think about that. If everyone, Manipulators and public alike bought at the bottom, who would be left to buy from us at the top? Buying at the bottom would do them no good unless they have someone to sell to at higher prices – and that is where you come in.

Most people, the investing public that is, only show faith when a stock is showing promise, when it is rallying, when there's lots of volume, lots of attention on it and, lots of volatility. This is why the Manipulators will always have someone to sell to at the top. We stay out when it's in the bottom range because there's nothing happening and then we buy in at the top when there's lots of action because we think we have a better chance of making more profit, more quickly. Can you see how this will lead to losses time and time again?

Somehow, someway, you must learn a new faith. After all, the definition of faith is "a belief in something before it happens - before you are offered tangible proof". Faith is believing in an outcome in advance of any signs of progress. This is the kind of faith you must be aware of, come to adopt, and put into practice. This is the faith of the Manipulators and all those who follow them. Hopefully, throughout the course of this book, you will come to acknowledge that this faith is your best chance at success in the markets.

You must learn to have faith in the price action that is revealed to you on your long term price charts. Have faith that a long, quiet period of inactivity, an accumulation base, is opportunity hiding. You must learn to tune out the part of your brain that tells you there must be something wrong with it if it has been down in the lower price range for so long. You must see through their tricks and realize this is exactly what they want you to think, to get you out at the bottom or to keep you from getting in at the bottom.

In fact, the longer and more quiet the base, the more of your attention it should draw. You must believe that these long bases are the sign posts leading you to your next opportunity, the keys to unlocking your next treasure chest. This is the simple truth about the markets. This is what THEY don't want you to know.

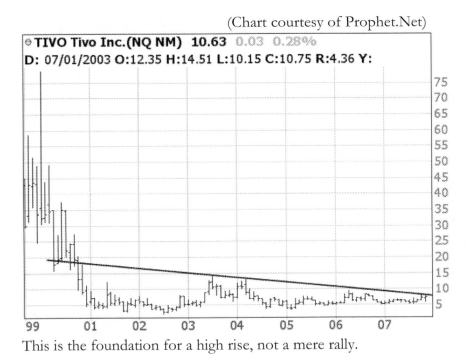

(Chart courtesy of Prophet.Net)

TIVO Tivo Inc.(NQ NM) 10.63 0.03 0.28%
D: 07/01/2003 O:12.35 H:14.51 L:10.15 C:10.75 R:4.36 Y:

This is the foundation for a high rise, not a mere rally.

After having completed its most recent price cycle in 2000, Tivo has spent the better part of the last 7 years trading under $10. This is the kind of discouraging action that should grab your attention.

The very best way to gain this faith is to study and practice. Follow and track as many stocks as you can in your free time. Examine chart after chart after chart. Gain the confidence you need to follow these signs. The more you study - the more you will reinforce your belief. The more that you rely on yourself and your price charts for all the information you need - the more successful you will become. Develop unquestioning confidence, and you will never look back. As Ted Warren said, "instead of asking your broker for a good stock, ask your broker for a sound company whose stock price has been in the bottom range for some time." This is where you'll find the real bargains.

There is a quote I heard from Ken Roberts that goes something like this. "You may pay a high price for the advice of a market expert for he can offer you but one opinion. On the daily price charts every day, are the opinions of thousands of people, who back up those opinions with cold hard cash."

Think about what this means. Everything that is going on in the market (in the world for that matter) and how it is being interpreted by traders, how it factors into their decision making process and to what extent, is revealed to you on the price charts. Whether they buy, sell, hold and at what prices they do this, is all right in front of your eyes.

Why would you want to limit yourself to just one or two opinions? On the price chart you can find everything in one place. Every news item, financial statistic, market or economy effect is considered by those trading and then the result of those influences is factored into their decisions and then either acted upon or not. And, everything that is acted upon is there for you to see.

STOCK MARKET MYTH #2
<u>Past Action is Not Indicative of Future Performance</u>

All of this is valuable to you, only if you can come to believe that past action does, in fact, offer you evidence of future prospect. Most, if not all fundamentalists ** will vehemently oppose anyone who suggests that the past action of a stock is a window to the future.

Hopefully, after seeing what you will see, and reading what you will read, and being reinforced through your own continued practice, you will come to not only believe, but rely on this simple truth.

** A fundamentalist is someone who makes their investment decisions by trying to gather, decipher and then interpret mounds of data such as: price to earnings ratios, asset values, the companies products and how they compare to their competition, the soundness of the companies' balance sheet, their debt, lawsuits, government intervention, analysts' forecasts, earnings and projections for the future, global demand, consumer spending, interest rates, the value of the dollar, etc, etc....

Who can deny that the "smart money" buys low and sells high. Even the fundamentalists don't deny this. Well, if this is happening, then wouldn't it make sense that there would be some indication of it on every price chart? What else is a price chart other than a representation of all the trades that take place on a daily, weekly, and monthly basis?

Wouldn't all that buying in the bottom range by the smart money be represented as the quiet sideways price action that we see on so many charts? And, if we know that they buy low and then sell high, then who can deny that the price chart not only offers a view of what has happened in the past, but also the most accurate picture of what is about to happen in the future.

Aren't they called the smart money because they buy low and sell high? Well, if there is a lot of quiet sideways activity in the lower range then doesn't that mean that prices have to rise from here in order for them to sell higher so they can then later be referred to as "smart". Surely even the fundamentalists must agree with this logic. Then what we are referring to as accumulation (this quiet, sideways action in the bottom range) is exactly that – a launching pad for higher prices, a base from which prices will rise, a level from which the smart money (the Manipulators) start to earn profits from.

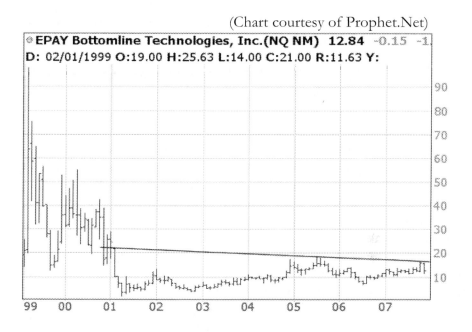

EPAY Bottomline Technologies, Inc.(NQ NM) 12.84 ~0.15 ~1.
D: 02/01/1999 O:19.00 H:25.63 L:14.00 C:21.00 R:11.63 Y:

They have a plan, and the longer prices stay in the accumulation phase, the better their plan is working. There are a number of reasons why they are able to pull this off.

1. they have the resources to back them up
2. they have lots of time because they have the resources
3. they know that the investing public is impatient and wants quick results
4. they know that if they stick to their plan they will prosper because what has worked in the past will work again in the future (Law of Cause & Effect)

How many of us start investing or trading with no plan at all? Or, if we have a plan, it changes as soon as prices go against us. And then later, we get onto a different plan altogether only to abandon it when it doesn't work.

The Manipulators are unified, confident, patient, and well financed. The public is disorganized, hopeful but unsure, impatient, and risking money they can't afford to lose.

Think about what we have just said, the public is impatient and risking money they can't afford to lose, while the Manipulators use discouraging price action over a long period of time with incredible resources to back them up. Is it any wonder why they are so successful at getting rid of the public in the bottom range?

The following chart of RF Micro Devices is a perfect example of discouraging action. All of 2003, 2004, 2005, 2006, and 2007 saw prices drift helplessly sideways and lower. The point is, however, that they were not helpless, they were helped. You will find the same type of discouraging action on almost any long term chart you look at. They all take different shapes and sizes but inevitably, some sort of discouraging action will precede every big move. You just have to know what to look for. Whenever prices look like they are flat lining for a period of years, you can be sure that the Manipulators are loading up. How do they do it, how do they keep prices so low for so long? It isn't difficult. It just takes patience and persistence. Once they are able to acquire enough shares during the latter stages of markdown and the early stages of accumulation, they then have all the power that they need to keep prices low and discouraging while they acquire all that they desire.

(Chart courtesy of Prophet.Net)

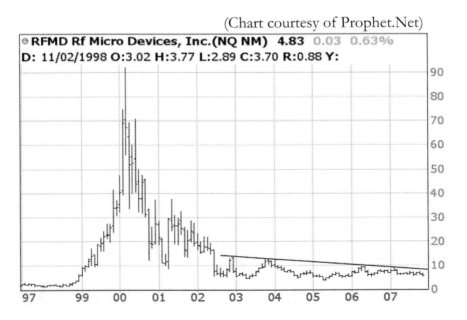

Again, the Manipulators' plan is one of unification and teamwork (one for all and all for one) whereas the investor's plan is, "I'm out for me and I don't care about anyone else." The whole process is really quite simple. They commit a large number of their shares to either the buy side of the equation (if they want to cause a rally or offer support to falling prices) or to the sell side of the equation (if they want a stop a rally in its tracks or encourage prices to fall back). And, the result of their work is represented by many years worth of quiet, discouraging price action on the long term chart. But, in order to show you how they do it, we will have to take a close up view to see what they are actually doing on a daily basis to make it all happen. Keep in mind though that this approach of manipulating prices is used throughout all phases of the price cycle.

For those of you who have day traded and watched the bid/ask in real time, you will already have a good grasp of what I'm talking about, but for those of you who haven't, I'll explain it here in a little more detail.

At any moment in time, for any stock, there are bid orders (people who want to buy stock at a price lower than where it is currently trading) and ask orders (people who want to sell some stock at a price higher than where it is currently trading). Market orders are used by people who either want to buy or sell at the current price.

Let's have a look at a typical bid/ask. The following chart is referred to as market depth. It shows all of the buy and sell orders, five layers deep, on either side of the stock's current price. Please note however, that this is a fluid indicator which changes constantly throughout the day as buy and sell orders are executed. We are just looking at a frozen moment in time for the purposes of our example.

Market Depth: Current Price: 2.68

		BID	ASK		
Orders	Volume	Price	Price	Volume	Orders
4	10,000	2.68	2.70	1,800	1
2	15,500	2.66	2.71	1,400	2
8	12,400	2.65	2.72	22,600	7
2	26,000	2.64	2.74	11,500	3
5	23,700	2.63	2.75	5,400	4

Once the Manipulators have bought up a sufficient number of shares, they gain control over prices. How? By loading the bid and ask sides of the equation, they can make prices do anything they want.

Prices are like a puppet on a string. They can hold them steady, incite a rally, stop it short in its tracks, induce a setback and then support it when they feel prices have gone low enough. Remember when we talked about accumulation and the two main goals of the Manipulators.

3. To keep you out, if you are not yet in AND,
4. to get you out, if you are already in.

Investors are a fickle bunch and will change their minds quickly and frequently. Refer to the bid/ask chart above. Right now there is a lot more support than resistance for this stock. Meaning that there are more shares wishing to be bought right now versus sold. There are four orders to purchase a combined 10,000 shares if prices drop to $2.68 and another two orders to purchase a combined 15,500 if prices drop to $2.66. On the other hand, at $2.70 and $2.71 there is a combined 3,200 shares for sale. If one buyer, or combination of buyers turned optimistic about this stock and wanted to get into this market right away, they would quickly eat through the available stock for sale at $2.70 and $2.71. And, depending on how many shares they all wanted to purchase at that time, they may even start to eat away at the 22,600 available at $2.72. Seeing this action, more investors may turn optimistic and buy because they think a good investment is a stock that is already moving. This helps the buyers to go through what's left at $2.72. As the last shares are purchased at the $2.72 level, buyers who still want to get in are now forced to pay $2.74 per share and so on. This is how prices rise (assuming there was not a significant enough increase in new sell orders as to slow or stop the buying move).

However, what if buying pressure soon thereafter subsided and prices were unable to rise any higher than $2.74? If enough investors turned pessimistic about this stock at the same time then they would start to sell down to the market. Some investors, who had placed ask orders at $2.74 and higher may now feel there is not enough optimism around this stock to get buyers to pay $2.74 per share (or more) so they may feel that they have to lower their selling price in order to get out before prices drop too far. Depending on the situation, they may lower their ask orders, or they may even sell down to the highest bid price to get out ASAP. For the purposes of this example let's assume that's still $2.68. If enough investors wanted to sell at the same time, they would eat through the available buy orders at $2.68 and then they would start working on those orders at $2.66 and so on (assuming there was not a significant enough increase in new buy orders as to slow or stop the selling move). This is how prices fall.

Because the Manipulators own so many shares, they simply have to keep adding sell orders to the ask side to keep prices from rising or buy orders to the bid side to keep prices from falling. In this way they are able to control prices in a tight range. All that it takes now is time - time for the public to become impatient and sell.

Remember, the Manipulators are in no hurry. They do not, nor can they acquire all that they wish to purchase in just a matter of a day or two, week or two, or even a month or two. Referring to the bid/ask chart above, let's say there are 50 million shares outstanding for this stock and the Manipulators' goal is to purchase a large percentage of them. This means that in order for them to reach their goal in a short period of time they would need to buy up shares by the hundreds of thousands every day. But, as you can see from the bid/ask, if they were to do this, they would simply overwhelm those shares available for sale. This buying pressure would drive prices so high so fast, that they would defeat their own purpose of trying to keep prices low, in order to increase the size of their position in the bottom range.

This is why they must take their time (years) and only buy up those shares that are being offered for sale by the public on a daily basis. That may mean that they can only purchase 10,000 or 20,000 or even 30,000 shares per day as the public slowly loses faith over time and sells down to the BID side. This is how they keep prices down and discouraging, while at the same time, accumulating millions of shares over time. Primarily, they accumulate on the BID side of the transaction, or in other words, when prices are falling.

The longer prices drift sideways and appear discouraging, the easier time they will have of controlling prices. Fewer and fewer investors will want to get involved in a stock that is displaying little activity, low volume, and little promise. As time drags on, the Manipulators don't have to worry too much about new investors entering the market at the bottom as much as they do about shaking out those who are still hanging on.

They continue to manipulate price movement in this manner day after day, week after week, month after month, year after year, and in the end, they slowly but surely accumulate a large position for themselves while worrying the majority of the public out at the bottom.

(Chart courtesy of Prophet.Net)

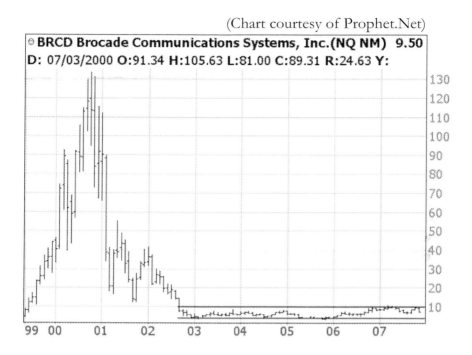

BRCD Brocade Communications Systems, Inc.(NQ NM) 9.50
D: 07/03/2000 O:91.34 H:105.63 L:81.00 C:89.31 R:24.63 Y:

Here you can see the result of the Manipulators actions. They are able to control the price movement of Brocade by loading the BID and ASK sides of the order desk – not allowing prices to fall below $3.50 and not allowing prices to rise above $10. And, as years pass, most investors grow impatient and eventually sell.

Now that you understand how easy it is for them to control prices, we'll have a look at how they use this ability over a longer period of time in order to achieve their fantastic results.

Price Patterns

The day by day, month by month, year by year price controlling activity of the Manipulators takes different forms and results in a variety of easily recognizable patterns or formations on the long term price chart. Just as each day may be discouraging on its own, string a number of these days together and the picture that results is a price display lacking energy and promise. The four formations that we'll discuss are the most widely seen patterns, however, they are by no means the only shapes that you will see on your long term charts. The fact that these four appear on so many charts though lends credence to their ability to get the job done for the Manipulators. By their very nature they are extremely discouraging and hence work time and time again to shake the public out in the bottom range. And, since they work with such proficiency and dependability, why would the Manipulators not use them over and over again?

Head & Shoulders

The head and shoulders formation is very discouraging to most investors because it offers the appearance that prices are unable to rise, therefore, prices must be weak. It is characterized by two upper boundaries with one large setback in between.

(Chart courtesy of Prophet.Net)

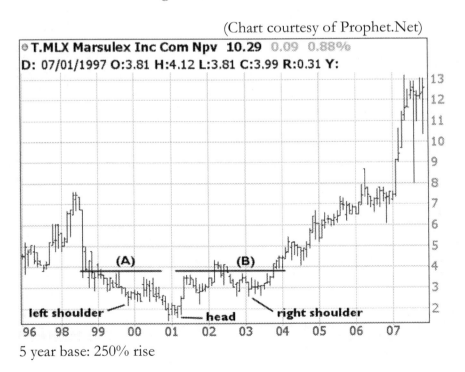

5 year base: 250% rise

Some head and shoulders formations will last a year, others up to 10 years or more, and it is these longer term price patterns that we are particularly interested in. The price action during a head and shoulders formation is very discouraging, which is the reason it works so well.

Referring to Marsulex (previous page), the public becomes discouraged as prices hit an invisible barrier (A), fall back, rally, and then hit that same barrier again, unable to break through to new highs (the U shaped setback underneath the barrier is known as the left shoulder). This appears to investors as a stock that can't seem to go any higher, therefore, they conclude it will likely go lower, so they sell. Of course, prices do fall back, this time to even lower lows than the first setback. This is known as the head. Now, even more investors are running for the exits for fear of bigger losses because they have no idea how low prices will go this time. The left shoulder and the head will usually discourage most of the public out of the market but for those who are still hanging on, or for those who are just getting into the market for the first time, the Manipulators have one more surprise in store. When prices finally do rally back to previous levels, they once again bump into that same invisible barrier (B) and fall back, rally and fall back again (the U shaped setback underneath the barrier is known as the right shoulder).

The Manipulators are conditioning your way of thinking. The more times that prices bump up against and fall back from that same level (false ceiling), the more this action creates for you a new, more intense perception. A perception that prices will not be able to go any higher, therefore they must be going lower. This becomes your new reality and this causes you to sell out at the bottom. This is why it's referred to as a false ceiling. Because even though it acts as an upper boundary through which prices cannot penetrate, this ceiling is in fact, only temporary in nature. Thus, if you can use this new found knowledge to change your perceptions, then that which seems so pessimistic to most, becomes an opportunity for those of us who are savvy to the ways of the Manipulators.

Unfortunately, the head and shoulders formation is difficult to detect until it is almost complete. This is why it's **always** wise to place your buy orders on the breakout of the price formation rather than trying to catch prices at their lowest point. A breakout simply refers to that point in time when prices are able to bust through an upper barrier such as the false ceiling (B) shown above.

If you were to try to catch the bottom with your buy order, and what you thought was a head and shoulders formation in the making turned out to be just a downtrend in price, you would surely be disappointed as prices would continue lower and lower. However, once the right shoulder starts to set up and a resistance level becomes apparent, you have confirmation and a signal as to where to enter your buy order. Buy on the breakout above the false ceiling of the right shoulder (B). For Marsulex, that would have been towards the end of 2003 when prices broke above the $3.80 level.

As you'll notice, head and shoulders formations usually appear towards the end of the accumulation phase just before prices are ready to begin markup. It is often times a last ditch effort for the Manipulators to discourage the last "hangers-on" out of the market prior to lift off. Sometimes, however, the head and shoulders formation will constitute the entire base as in the case of Ralph Lauren.

(Chart courtesy of Prophet.Net)

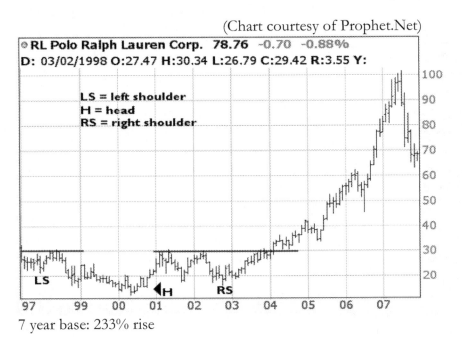

7 year base: 233% rise

"Stop-buys" are buy orders that are placed in advance with your broker or on your computer's trading platform such that when prices come up to the level were you want to get in, your buy order is triggered automatically. This allows you the flexibility of not having to wait and watch as prices trade up and down everyday. Most people don't have the opportunity to follow prices this closely, nor would I ever recommend that you do even if you do have the time.

Always remember the big picture. We are taking a price cycle perspective because that is what the Manipulators do. The more frequently you follow prices, the more your perceptions will gravitate back towards a "public" perspective. This will cause you to make incorrect decisions, which will get you out of sync with the Manipulators and back in sync with the rest of the investing public. And this will put you right back where you started, buying high and selling low or buying low and selling lower.

Looking at the Polo Ralph Lauren chart (previous page) - once you started to identify the false ceiling of the right shoulder setting up at $30 over the course of 2001, 2002 and then again in 2003, a stop-buy order placed in advance (let's say at $31), would have caught the breakout just right. You may not have been watching, or you may have even been away on vacation at the time, but your order would have been filled automatically. That's the beauty of the stop-buy.

Head and shoulders formations will take many shapes and sizes, but it is not their shape that is as important as what they are intended to do - to discourage you out in the bottom range.

In the case of Columbus McKinnon (next page), it is easy to see that the Manipulators were not satisfied with the size of their holding nor with the number of investors still in the market at the end of 2005. How can I know this? Because of the price action that followed. The four year head and shoulders base wasn't quite discouraging enough so the Manipulators employed a false start, followed by a final shakeout.

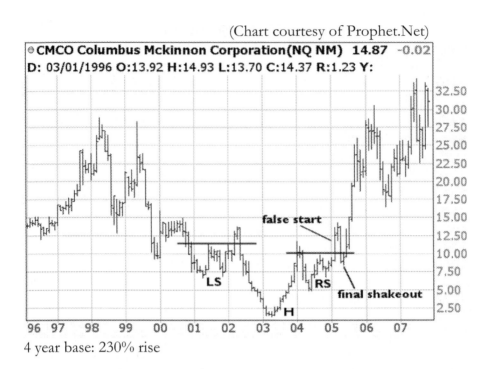

(Chart courtesy of Prophet.Net)

4 year base: 230% rise

A **false start** is characterized by prices making a quick jump up and out of a formation or through an upper resistance barrier only to fall back a short time later.

The false start got much of the public to believe that prices were finally on the move higher, but when prices quickly reversed direction and fell back below the $10 level, many who had just got in, got right back out with a loss. Then when prices proceeded higher again after the final shakeout, all those same investors were left on the sidelines, too nervous to enter for fear of a similar setback.

The reason it is called a **final shakeout** is because it tends to be the last major setback in price (during the end of accumulation or beginning of markup) just prior to a significant rise.

For Columbus Mckinnon, a stop-buy placed above $10 in late 2004 (after prices confirmed the resistance level of the right shoulder), would have been perfect to catch the impending markup phase.

The chart of Columbus McKinnon presents us with a great opportunity to talk about stops or as they are also quite commonly referred to as stop-losses, or stop-sell orders. These are sell orders placed in advance with a broker (or entered on your trading software platform) such that if prices fall back to a certain level your sell order will be triggered automatically, resulting in the closing out of your position. Many experts and brokers will recommend that you always use stops to avoid greater losses if prices move against you. I am going to challenge that way of thinking.

Now that you are aware of the BIG PICTURE, the man-made price cycle, and how each phase is connected to the others in a finely orchestrated sequence of Cause and Effect, why would you ever want to take a chance of being out of a market near the bottom after having just entered on the breakout of a large accumulation base? Now sure, prices may go against you for a time after entering, but with a price cycle perspective (having invested in a solid company), and with a solid base of many years behind you, you can hang on with confidence knowing that the Manipulators did not spend all of this time and effort for no return.

Sooner or later they will drive prices to much higher levels because it is the only way for them to profit. The only question is, will you have the patience and faith to go along for the ride?

Of course there are situations when companies will fail and your loss will be realized. However, this is when your due diligence ahead of time comes into play in order to reduce the likelihood of this happening. As we'll discuss in a later section, stop-sells do have their place when it comes time to sell, but not until prices have made their way into the markup phase and/or on into distribution, after having made significant gains. But, when used in the bottom range during accumulation and early markup, stop-sells will more often than not cause you to be shaken out of the market right before it rallies to <u>significant new highs</u>.

In the case of Columbus McKinnon, your stop buy order would have been triggered during the false start above $10 in early '05. Had you placed a stop-sell order after entering the market it would surely have been triggered when prices dropped sharply from their new highs of about $14 in 2005 down to under $10 one month later during the final shakeout.

In this example, you may have even managed a small profit had you entered on the breakout of the right shoulder just above $10 and sold before prices fell back too far. However, would this really have been a success if you then found yourself out of the stock and watching from the sidelines as prices continued their run up to $30 over the course of the next year?

Now that you know why prices move the way they do, you can look at setbacks and final shakeouts as good and necessary price action for the purposes of sustaining a steady and consistent markup phase.

The greater the number of public investors that are left on the sidelines, or are shaken out during accumulation and markup, the longer the Manipulators will retain control and the higher prices will ultimately go. However, if you find yourself out of the market because your stop was triggered during a setback or final shakeout, you will never be around to cash in on the really big moves that are the inevitable result of large accumulation bases.

You must study and practice as much as it takes in order to build your faith, because your success depends upon it.

STOCK MARKET MYTH #3
You Can't Go Broke Taking Profits

The truth is… this is how most investors do go broke.

Without an awareness of the Manipulated price cycle, the public is left to believe that every rally is good and every setback is bad. So, it is best to sell and take profits at the first sign of trouble (after prices have rallied in their favour) or, to limit losses when prices fall back right after entering a market. Unfortunately, without a price cycle perspective and insight into why prices act the way they do, the public never gains the confidence to ride a markup to higher highs. And ultimately get shaken out at the first sign of "apparent" trouble cutting off their ability to ever realize significant gains. This "limiting of profits approach" only serves to cap their gains to the upside to the same degree they are capping their losses to the downside.

This is no way to accumulate wealth, 1 step forward, 1 step back, 1 step forward, 1 step back. How many of you have looked back at your accounts after a year to realize that you weren't making any real progress? When you did make a few good profits, there always seemed to be a few good losses to go right along with them and in the end you felt you were doing well just by managing to keep your account from decreasing in size. Holding steady now became your new reality. You felt if you could just hold steady for a while, you would hit that one really good trade and your account would be propelled to the next level. But what happened? Just when you thought you had made a great pick, prices set back and your new profit started to quickly evaporate. You either sold right away to lock-in a small profit out of fear that prices would continue lower, or you hung on until your profit turned into a loss and then you sold out of fear that a small loss would become a larger loss.

Your inability to see the big picture, the man-made price cycle, caused you to sell out of fear on the downside and out of fear on the upside. Can you see how you have backed yourself into a corner — how you have set a pre-defined boundary for every trade you make?

If you've never made a significant profit on a stock in the past (200% − 800%), chances are you never will in the future either. Why? Because you either are not aware of WHY prices move they way they do or if you are, you haven't practiced enough to build the kind of faith you need to see you through these inevitable ups and downs of accumulation and early markup.

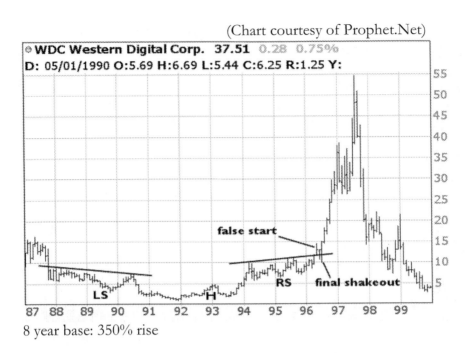

8 year base: 350% rise

Western Digital is another example of a head and shoulders base, but this time with shoulders slanted on an angle. Again, the shape of the base, or the position of the resistance levels is not what's most important. The fact that prices traded in a discouraging manner under $10 for many years is what we focus our attention on. It is the building up of this strong base that signals an opportunity.

A stop-buy placed above $12 (the breakout level of the right shoulder) would have been filled in early '96 during the false start and forced you to carry a loss for the next month or two as prices setback below the right shoulder. However, with a strong base behind you, you would have again had the faith to hang on and wait for the inevitable markup phase to begin, which it did just 2 months later. The important thing is you would have spotted this opportunity, placed your stop-buy once you identified the resistance level of the right shoulder, been patient as prices moved against you during the final shakeout, and still been in as prices then proceeded higher. And proceed higher they did, to the tune of about 350%. Had you been using a stop-sell after entering this market, you would have likely been stopped out during the setback below $12, and then watched from the sidelines as another stock rose to all time highs without you.

NOTE: Why was Western Digital falling during 1998 and 1999 when many of the well known DOW and NASDAQ components were racing their way to all time highs during one of the biggest "bull" markets in history (to use their terminology)? Did someone forget to tell them?

No, they were simply following their own man-made price cycle as all stocks do. 1998 and 1999 just happened to coincide with the markdown phase for this stock after having already risen over 350% from its base.

Do you think the Manipulators care that many of the big name stocks were making tremendous gains while WDC was falling in price from $50 back down to $10? Of course not - they had just finished cashing out for huge profits and now that prices were back below $10, it was time to start accumulating another position, to prepare for the next markup phase. This is just a little reminder to you that there is no such thing as a BULL or BEAR market. There are simply accumulations, markups, distributions, and markdowns of individual stocks.

Remember, regardless of where you draw your line of resistance for the right shoulder and enter this market, the fact that you entered is what is important, not at what price.

Buying and selling will always be an inexact science, however, if you can maintain a price cycle perspective, when all is said and done, you will be much further ahead than when you started.

NOTE: Often times the head and shoulders formation will not make up the entire base on its own, but rather be just one part of many years worth of boring, depressing accumulation action. It is the entire base which gives this stock its strength to rise. The head and shoulders formation merely adds to it, and most importantly, offers us a signal as to where to enter the market so as to put us that much closer to the beginning of the markup phase and profits.

<u>Channels</u>

When prices trade sideways within a tight range for a period of time we refer to it as a channel. When a channel extends for a number of years in the bottom range, we refer to it as a channeling base.

The price action that is taking place within a channel is extremely discouraging and worrisome to investors. Even though prices are well supported and are not able to go lower than their downside support, they are also not able to make any headway above their upside resistance barrier. Without headway, progress, or some kind of encouraging movement to the upside to give the public a reason to hang on, it's just a matter of time until they lose faith and sell. And, since the Manipulators are in no hurry for that specific reason, you can see how prices, (after channeling) for many years, will cause even the most optimistic of shareholders to eventually sell out. Time and discouraging price action will always work at shaking the public out at the bottom and these two factors are perhaps nowhere better observed, than in a channeling base.

(Chart courtesy of Prophet.Net)

LOW Lowe's Companies Inc 21.17 0.23 1.10%
D: 01/02/1975 O:0.1961 H:0.2279 L:0.1713 C:0.2208 R:0.0566 Y:

false start

75 77 78 79 80 81 82 83 84 85 86 87 88 89 90 91 92 93 94 95 96 97 98

18 yr base: 3346% rise from 1992 – 2007 (not all shown)

After flat lining for the first 8 years, prices for Lowe's (previous page) traded in the $0.50 to $1.00 range for next 10 years, until finally breaking out of their channel in 1992 for the last time. By simply loading the bid side of the equation every time prices dropped towards $0.50, the Manipulators were able to support prices and keep them from falling further. By loading the ask side of the equation every time prices rallied up to $1.00, the Manipulators were able to stall prices and keep them from going higher. In this way, they were able to keep prices down and discouraging for 18 years. Prices appeared weak and unable to go higher. The result - the Manipulators added to their position and strength as the public lost faith and sold.

Had you placed a stop-buy order in the late 80's to enter this market when prices broke out above the $1.00 false ceiling, you would have been filled, and then quickly disappointed as prices made their way right back down into the channel for the next 18 months. Would you have had the patience to hang on? A savvy investor with a "price cycle perspective" would have. A false start and setback do not change the reason you got into this market in the first place. Lowe's had set up a strong 16 year base to that point, and you knew that markup would have to occur sooner or later. This is just a case where it happened to occur a little later. However, the fact remains that you would have still profited to the same degree as the investor who entered on the subsequent breakout above $1.00 at the beginning of 1992.

Sometimes the Manipulators will trick even those of us who are aware of their practices (i.e., the timing of our buys and sells). But, they cannot change the overall nature of their practice which is to mark prices to much higher levels after having accumulated a large holding for themselves in the bottom range. It is, after all, the only way for them to profit. If you can develop Manipulator-like patience, you are well on your way.

(Chart courtesy of Prophet.Net)

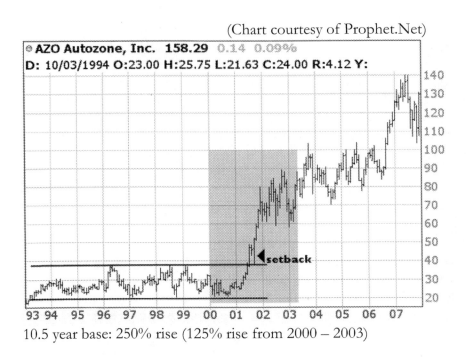

AZO Autozone, Inc. 158.29 0.14 0.09%
D: 10/03/1994 O:23.00 H:25.75 L:21.63 C:24.00 R:4.12 Y:

10.5 year base: 250% rise (125% rise from 2000 – 2003)

Autozone traded between $20 and $39 for 8.5 years before breaking up and out of its channel. Some channels will develop in just a few years while others set up for 10 – 20 years or more. Again it is solely based on what the Manipulators need in order to accomplish their goal in this phase of the price cycle. In this case, the Manipulators must have been quite successful at worrying the majority of the public out of the market because they proceeded with markup after only 8.5 years of accumulation. A stop-buy placed above $39 would have put you into this market in mid 2001 and into profits immediately.

A setback followed almost immediately after breakout with prices re-tracing back down to $39 after having just reached new highs at about $49. This is a great example of why I caution you against using stop-losses in the very earliest stages of markup. Even though this represented a 20% drop in prices ($49 to $39), what may seem like a prudent strategy will more often than not leave you on the sidelines holding a small profit (or loss) and watching as prices turn and make their way hundreds of percent higher. Setbacks immediately following breakouts only delay that which is inevitable – markup.

(Chart courtesy of Prophet.Net)

CRRC Courier Corporation(NQ NM) 15.27 -0.05 -0.33%
D: 05/02/1988 O:0.8607 H:0.9004 L:0.768 C:0.821 R:0.1324 Y:

23 yr base (not all shown): 2200% rise to $46 in 2006 (not shown)
(300% rise from 2000-2003)

Referring to Courier Corp., notice how prices, after breaking out from their base in 1994, traded in a very tight range just above the $2.00 level. And then, when prices made their way up to new highs in 1995, fell right back to $2.00, where they were again supported. This practice of resistance turned support is widely used, especially during the beginning stages of markup in an attempt to trigger as many stop-loss orders as possible.

Most investors are unaware of the price cycle and therefore believe that all setbacks are bad. With the fear of lost profits tugging away at them, they inevitably protect their profits at the first sign of trouble and are once again left to sit on the sidelines and watch as prices markup to all time highs.

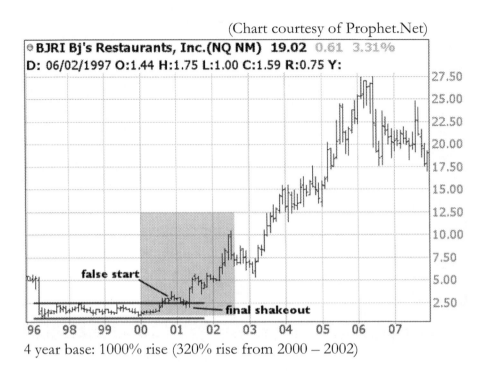

(Chart courtesy of Prophet.Net)

4 year base: 1000% rise (320% rise from 2000 – 2002)

Only a long term chart like this one can tell you if you are really buying in the bottom range. Eleven years of price history for Bj's Restaurant's reveals all time lows during its 4 year channeling base. How many public investors would have been able to hang on through this depressing lack of energy? Not many as evidenced by the high rise to follow. Remember, each phase has a Cause and Effect relationship with the phase preceding it. In this case, the "effect" (or result) being markup and its "cause" being that of accumulation.

Buying on the breakout of this formation would have been an easy call to make back in mid 2000. Look at the final shakeout that occurred in 2001. Final shakeouts are commonplace and are very useful for those of us who are aware of "WHY" they take place in the first place. Doesn't it seem kind of funny that a company whose business is apparently doing well enough to have their stock on the verge of rising to all time highs, would all of a sudden see their stock price fall sharply by 40 - 50% just prior to that rise - quite a coincidence?

What changed so dramatically about the company to account for that freefall to $2.00, only to then see it turn around and rise 300% within the next 15 months, and then never look back on its way to all time highs of $27.50? Nothing fundamentally important changed about the business – it's simply a tool the Manipulators use to trick the public into making wrong decisions.

For those of us who are aware of their methods, however, rather than this being a disappointing situation, it actually provides us with crucial information. A sharp shakeout is an almost sure sign that markup is close at hand, especially when it comes at the end of a long accumulation base. And, especially after prices have traded quietly, banging up against a long term resistance level such as the one seen here for Bj's at $2.50.

(Chart courtesy of Prophet.Net)

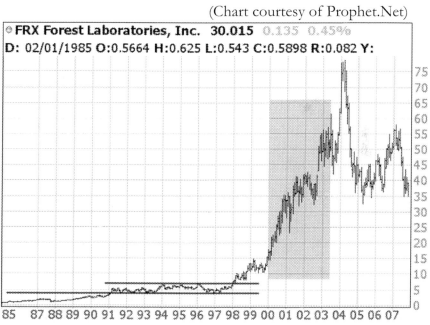

12 year base: 900% rise (233% rise from 2000 – 2003)

The name of the game in accumulation is quiet, sideways and discouraging. This 12 year channeling base for Forest Laboratories displays all of that and more. "More", meaning the result of what this depressing action does to shareholders. How many investors would have turned their attention away from this stock after seeing the depressing lack of energy during the 1990's? How many investors who had entered this market during 1994 or 1995 or 1996 would have been able to hang on through this seemingly helpless drift in prices? Your answer is also right there on the chart. If the Manipulators require the majority of the public out of the market prior to lift-off, then this channeling base obviously worked very well for them. After breaking out in 1998, prices never looked back. Your stop-buy placed in advance above the channel would have been triggered at about $8.00 leaving you with your hardest decision, when to sell.

(Chart courtesy of Prophet.Net)

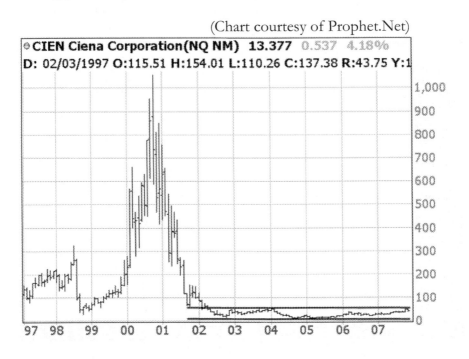

This 6 year channel for Ciena Corp. is extremely discouraging – to most of the public that is. To price cycle savvy investors this is a diamond in the rough, an opportunity in hiding, a foundation preparing to support a high rise. No matter what is happening with the stock market indices or the economy in general, there are many opportunities just like this one waiting to be uncovered. It's up to you to search them out and then be ready to act when the time is right.

Downtrending Bases

The downtrending base is successfully used over and over by Manipulators to frighten the public out prior to markup. And, as in all bases, the action appears weak, quiet and boring. Now add to that a slow, steady decline in price over many years and you have the making of an extremely demoralizing situation - one in which most investors have very little patience for. Those who are in get out, and those who are watching from the sidelines look elsewhere for more promise, more encouraging price action – trapped again.

The characteristic pattern is represented by a series of lower highs over a period of many years. Just as in the case of the head and shoulders formation, a downtrending base may account for the entire base on its own or it may represent just one part of a much larger, longer accumulation period. In either case, it has the desired effect the Manipulators strive for – to shake you out at the bottom or to keep you from getting in, in the first place.

(Chart courtesy of Prophet.Net)

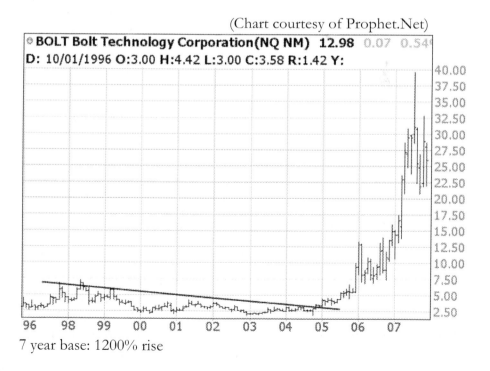

7 year base: 1200% rise

Look at how the price of Bolt Technology (previous page) drifted ~~helplessly,~~ or should I say, helped to go lower and lower, quieter and quieter for 7 years. Not many investors would have the heart to hang in there during this depressing price display. Add to that any number of negative news items and bad earnings reports along the way, and you have a perfect recipe for accumulation.

However, now that you are aware of what accumulation represents and why prices must trade like this for years before any significant rise takes place, you only need uncover these bases "in the making" and then patiently wait for markup to begin. A stop-buy order placed in advance at approx. $3.00 would have been triggered in late 2004 resulting in a large profit in a very short period of time. Again, your hardest decision would have been how much money to take off the table. We'll talk about this more in a later section.

(Chart courtesy of Prophet.Net)

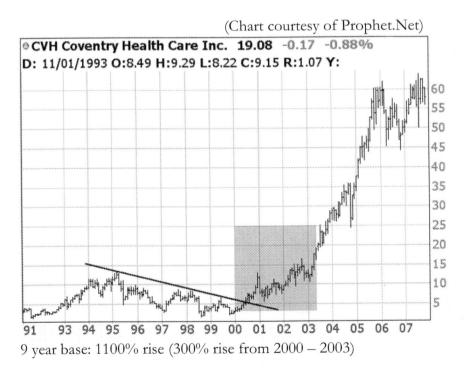

9 year base: 1100% rise (300% rise from 2000 – 2003)

These are the types of bases and opportunities that all price cycle savvy investors hope to uncover. Nine years worth of down-trending prices for Coventry (previous page) indicates a launching pad for a very large markup phase to follow. Your stop-buy order would have been triggered in mid 2000 at approx. $5.00.

Coventry Health Care is yet another stock that was unaware of the "BEAR" market that started in early 2000. Not only did prices not fall, along with the magical DOW, or even hold steady for that matter, but they in fact skyrocketed 300%, taking off at almost the exact time the DOW and NASDAQ began their plunge. How can we account for this? Very simply, the market in general has nothing to do with how individual stocks perform. A stock's performance is based solely on the size and strength of its base.

(Chart courtesy of Prophet.Net)

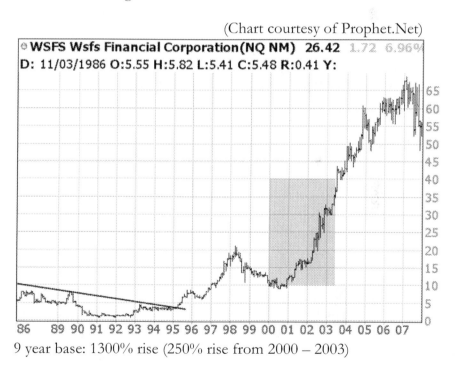

WSFS Wsfs Financial Corporation(NQ NM) 26.42 1.72 6.96%
D: 11/03/1986 O:5.55 H:5.82 L:5.41 C:5.48 R:0.41 Y:

9 year base: 1300% rise (250% rise from 2000 – 2003)

WSFS Financial shows us a very sound base. Notice the extremely quiet price action (during the last half of '93 and throughout all of '94) that preceded the breaking of the downtrending base in 1995. This is one last attempt to trick the public out prior to lift-off. A stop-buy placed above this point would have been triggered and caught the markup just right.

A downtrending base can also be looked upon merely as a down sloping trend line, which when broken offers up a buy signal.

A trend line is a line that connects the highs when prices are falling or the lows when prices are rising.

It is important to show, however, that the distinction I'm making between the two is the slope of the line. Depending on the rate of speed at which prices are falling, down trend lines can end up being quite steep. And, even though prices will eventually break through these lines to the upside, these situations do not necessarily represent good buying opportunities. Harvest Natural Resources illustrates this point very well.

(Chart courtesy of Prophet.Net)

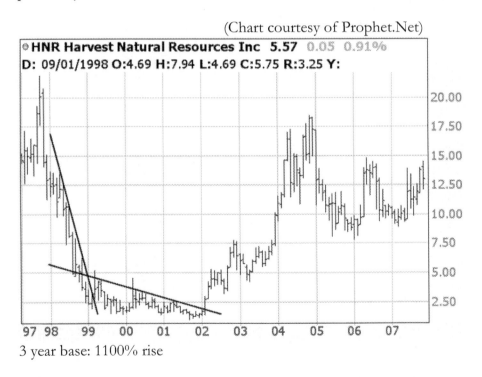

3 year base: 1100% rise

Buying on the break of the steep trend line in early 1999 would have produced a quick profit albeit a very temporary one unless you had the foresight to sell before prices fell back below your entry point.

We know that any significant rise in price requires the majority of the public to be sold out of the market and the only way that this can happen is if the Manipulators have enough time (years) to use discouraging price action to their benefit to accomplish this goal. A breakout to the upside of a steep down trend line therefore is more an indication of when the markdown phase is completing and when accumulation is beginning rather than a point at which you might enter your buy order. To this point, prices had spent very little time at the bottom, and the Manipulators did not have a chance to do what they needed to do to prepare this stock for a sustained rise. Therefore, you can see why steep trend lines are far less reliable as a means of determining when to enter a market.

On the other hand, a much flatter trend line such as the one seen spanning 1999 - 2001 allows for prices to trade at the bottom in a very discouraging manner for years. The breakout to the upside of this line identifies the completion of the accumulation phase and the beginning of the next markup phase, and therefore provides a much more reliable indicator of where to place your stop-buy order. I have used the term downtrending BASE for a reason. A BASE refers to years worth of quiet, discouraging price action in the bottom range. With a steep down trend line, there is very little base whatsoever.

(Chart courtesy of Prophet.Net)

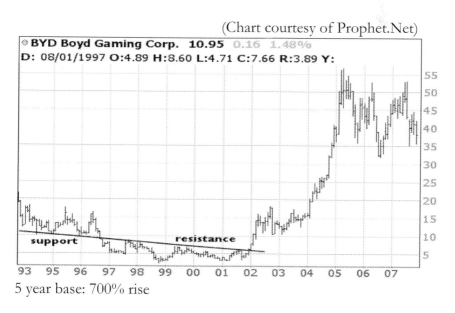

5 year base: 700% rise

(Chart courtesy of Prophet.Net)

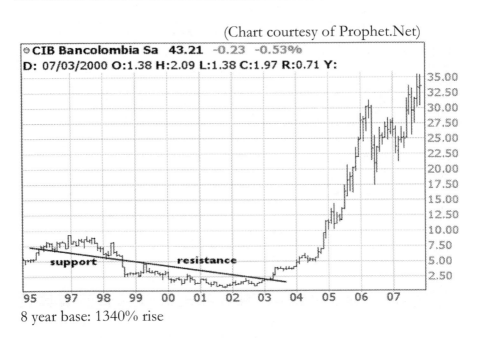

8 year base: 1340% rise

Boyd Gaming (previous page) and Bancolombia have a few things in common. They both have multi-year accumulation bases behind them. And, they are both presently involved in distribution having made significant gains over the course of 3 years. The other commonality is that they both demonstrate strong lines of support and resistance.

Often times prices will trade around an invisible barrier treating it as support during the markdown phase, resistance during the accumulation phase, and then in some cases, support again during markup. When these lines show up in connection with an accumulation, you can be even more sure of accurately identifying the resistance level of the base, and therefore have more confidence in placing your stop-buy to catch the beginning of markup just right. Many times investors will have trouble identifying the resistance level of a base. This lack of confidence will be just enough to keep them from placing their buy order, and as a result, they'll be left on the sidelines watching as prices mark up higher and higher. Therefore, be aware and on the lookout for these invisible lines of support and resistance. They will greatly improve your ability to identify the MOST accurate point at which a breakout may occur.

When drawing trend lines, the most accurate line will tend to be the one that has the most touch points. Or, in other words, the line that connects the most highs and/or lows of the preceding price action.

The most important thing to remember from this though is not WHERE to get in but rather TO GET IN. The exact entry point is not nearly as important as your ability to identify a strong base, and then act when it appears that prices are breaking up and out of a long period of accumulation. In as much as we use the trend lines as a means to identify where to place our buy orders, we should not let opportunities get away because we're not sure of exactly where to enter. The fact that the Manipulators have taken many years to shake the public out at the bottom is what defines this opportunity for us, not the location of where we happen to draw lines on the page. It is always better to be in a good opportunity and having to wait a little longer for profits because you didn't time the breakout just right, than to be on the sidelines watching, trying to time your entry point perfectly and possibly missing out on the opportunity altogether.

This will be the case with all formations and price patterns. We are using lines to help define entry and exit points and to try to minimize our waiting time to profits, however, never lose sight of the big picture - the WHY of prices. Never lose sight of why prices have been at the bottom for so long and why they then must rise significantly from these levels.

Flat-Top Triangles

Flat-top triangles are one of the most prevalent formations that you will see on your long term price charts. They are also referred to as ascending triangles, or pennants or false ceilings because they take the shape of a wedge with a flat top. The wedge takes shape as the result of a series of higher lows with rallies to the upside bumping up against a flat-top resistance level or false ceiling. I refer to these horizontal resistance levels as false ceilings because for a while they appear to be ceilings through which prices are unable to rise. However, prices do eventually break through, thereby proving them to be, in fact, false or temporary resistance levels.

Regardless of the name however, they all produce the same result – a perception amongst the public that prices are unable to rise above a certain level, therefore they must be weak. The public who are on the sidelines watching, look elsewhere for other opportunities showing more promise, more strength. And those who are already shareholders come to believe that prices cannot go up therefore their only choice is to sell before they go down.

In the case of Champion Industries, with a long term price chart in hand, it is very easy to spot the flat-top (false ceiling) at approx. $2.60 between 2000 and 2003. For some unknown reason to the public, prices were unable to make their way above this level. After 4 years of demoralizing action, they had all but given up and sold. On the flip side, the Manipulators had patiently waited while the public, one by one, offered up their shares for sale. The Manipulators obligingly bought them up and continued to grow their position in the bottom range. By the middle of 2003 they had worn out, frustrated, discouraged, and frightened the majority of the public shareholders out of this market, and with that, came complete control over prices and a readiness to mark prices up to higher levels.

(Chart courtesy of Prophet.Net)

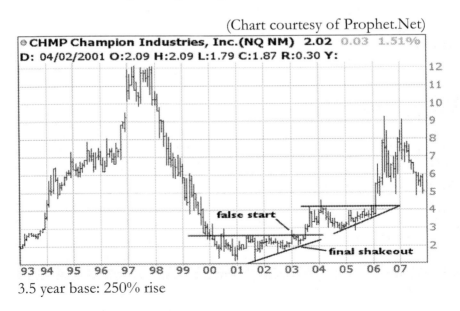

3.5 year base: 250% rise

After a false start in January 2003, prices setback to $2.00 (final shakeout) before rallying up and through the $2.60 barrier for the last time. Even though this shakeout stayed within the flat-top triangle formation, it must have had the desired effect the Manipulators were looking for because prices never looked back after that. During the markup stage, you can see how they employed a flat-top triangle at $4.25 also in order to discourage the public from getting in prior to moving prices to even higher levels. We'll talk more about techniques (and tricks) used during the markup phase in more detail, in the next section.

(Chart courtesy of Prophet.Net)

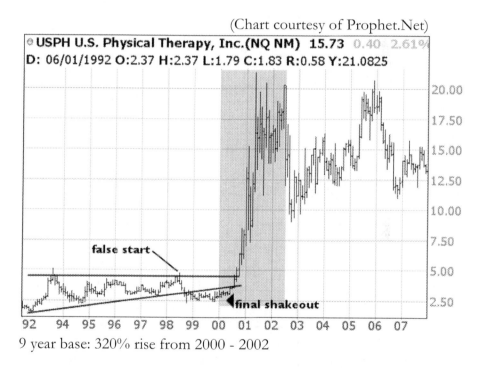

9 year base: 320% rise from 2000 - 2002

A 9 year flat-top triangle a prime candidate and would have been at the top of your watch list back in the late 90's. For US Physical Therapy, the final shakeout was long and low and discouraging (1998 – 2000), however, had you had the patience to either hold, (had you bought during the false start) or to wait for prices to rally back and then break through the flat-top at $4.75, your stop-buy order would have caught the breakout just right. Unlike Champion (previous page), this time the final shakeout came outside of the base formation, but in both cases, the goal of getting rid of the public was achieved and prices were then able to move higher. Make note also of how the line of support for the bottom of the triangle changed to resistance for the 2 year shakeout - more evidence of Manipulation and confirmation for you, when it comes time to place your buy order.

(Chart courtesy of Prophet.Net)

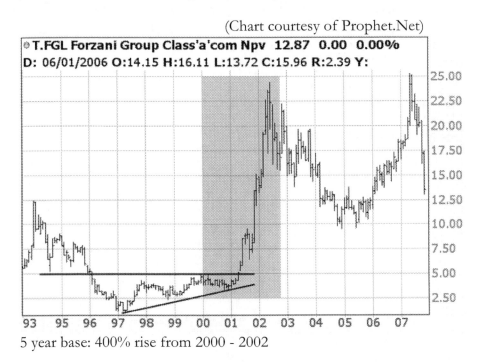

5 year base: 400% rise from 2000 - 2002

Beware of information, advice and news from the so-called "market experts" or media. Things are not always as they appear. Remember when we talked about how most people tend to choose a telephoto view of the world around them. However, when they change to a normal setting they reveal so much more that was previously hidden. And then when they go one step further and remove the camera from in front of their eyes altogether, they unveil a huge panorama which was always there, but which they were unable to see. Well, the same is true for most experts and media personnel. They tend to focus on the up close, the short term and hence base their advice on only a very narrow field of view.

For example, when these TV personalities highlight a stock and comment on the latest news affecting a company, they will usually follow it up with a price chart showing what has happened to prices over the course of the past 6 12 months. If the news is positive, and the prospects for this company going ahead appear good, then a chart like the one below for Celgene Corp. reveals what appears to be a real bargain. Prices have fallen 20% from their recent highs of $75.

(Chart courtesy of Prophet.Net)

Well, not so fast, remember what appears to be a bargain may not be a bargain after all. When we step back and reveal the huge panorama of information that is available to us, we see a whole new perspective – the "Price Cycle" perspective.

The 20 year chart of Celgene (next page) reveals that prices are clearly in the distribution phase after having risen over 2900% off the bottom. And we all know what follows distribution. Does $60 still look like a bargain? Prices were a bargain when they were breaking out of their base back in 1999, but they're certainly not a bargain now.

(Chart courtesy of Prophet.Net)

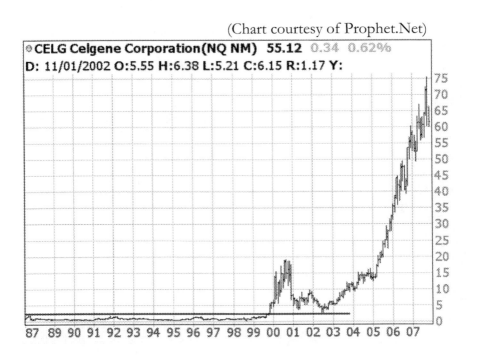

Look at the extremely quiet base for Celgene during the period from 1987 – 1999. Prices traded in a tight range under their $2.50 flat-top barrier. A stop-buy placed in advance would have been triggered in 1999 and turned into profits immediately. Again, your biggest problem would have been to know how long to hang on. We'll discuss selling opportunities and rationale, as well as adding to your position a little later. For now, come to have faith in two very important concepts (1) that a discouraging base of many years in the bottom range, no matter what the shape, produces the same result time and time again, and (2) the only way to really know if a stock is trading at a bargain is to view its long term price chart (10 - 20+ years worth of price history, if available).

Generally speaking, the longer the base - the stronger the base, however, as we have seen, that is not always the case. Sometimes a smaller 3 year base will produce a large 800% rise, whereas a much larger base of 10 years or more may only result in a smaller 200% rise. There are no absolutes when it comes to investing, however, with that said, I would still tend to count on a larger, longer base as having a greater chance of producing a larger rise than that of a smaller base. A lot of times the extent of the rise off the bottom will depend on what happens to prices during markup.

Investing in the equity markets will always be an inexact science. However, where you can count on some exactness is in the fact that markup follows accumulation, distribution follows markup, markdown follows distribution, and accumulation follows markdown, and so on...

The time it will take for a base to complete, the time it will take for prices to rise to the distribution phase, and the percentage gain of that rise will always vary, but the price cycle will remain the one constant that you can always count on. I have illustrated four of the most widely seen price patterns that occur on your long term price charts.

Again, keep in mind it is not the specific shape of the formation or where we draw or lines of support and resistance but rather what affect the boring, sideways, price action has on the investing public.

Whether it's a head and shoulders formation, a channel, a downtrending base or a flat-top triangle, if the price action is quiet and discouraging over the course of many years in the bottom range, then you have a price display that could only be interpreted as one thing - accumulation. From there, it's just a matter of when and where to place your buy order to enter the market and hitch a ride on the inevitable markup phase.

Placing buy orders on the breakout of large accumulation bases in the bottom range will give you the very best chance of success in the equity markets.

(Chart courtesy of Prophet.Net)

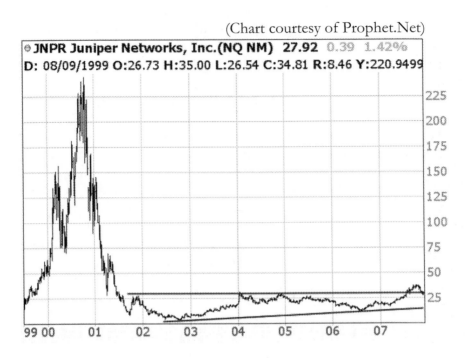

So far Juniper has set up a 6.5 year base under $30. This is the kind of base that you need you be on the lookout for because this is the kind of foundation that will support a "high rise".

If you can become adept at recognizing these quiet, discouraging accumulation patterns on your long term price charts, you will literally uncover treasure map after treasure map. Your next step then is to take on the challenges and obstacles along the path leading to your next treasure chest – this path is called the **markup phase.**

Mark-Up Phase

What happens when the Manipulators have discouraged the majority of the investing public out of a particular stock?

They are ready to start moving prices into higher territory.

Remember, it doesn't do them any good to spend all this time and effort and money unless they have a plan to profit from their investment, and believe me they do have a plan and it works with precision each and every time they put it into action. You would think that having invested all that effort and all that time (3, 5 or even 10 years or more), that they may be losing patience and be anxious to turn a quick profit. Well, not so fast.

If there is one thing that separates the Manipulators from the rest of us is that they never lose patience. You will come to understand the psychology that comes into play during this building process.

First we must go back to faith and confidence. Most people show faith in something only after it is showing promise. Well, this so-called faith is what fuels the markup phase. Prices gather strength and speed as they rise.

The Manipulators know full well that the vast majority of the public are not interested is something that lies quietly at the bottom showing no promise – no hope. This is why during the accumulation period they are so successful at keeping prices low, driving a large percentage of the public out of the market, and building a large position for themselves.

Well then, doesn't it follow that once prices start to rise off the bottom that some of the public will start to get interested and slowly enter the market themselves? What we have to keep in mind is what the Manipulators are attempting to do. Obviously, they want to drive prices up as high as they can, sell out all of their holdings and make as much profit as possible. But how do they go about doing this?

Remember when we talked about the reasons for keeping the public out at the bottom. One of those reasons was so that the Manipulators would have someone to sell to at the top. Well, the early stages of the markup are still a long way from the top. The Manipulators want to keep the majority of the public out until prices are much higher. That will enable them to unload the majority of their holdings in the higher price range.

To better understand this concept think of it in terms of a base runner attempting to steal second base. Doesn't the runner on first try to inch his way out as far as possible towards second base without the pitcher noticing, because he knows that the closer he is to second base when he starts running, the greater the chance he will have to slide in safely before the catcher has time to throw him out.

The same is true for the markup phase of a stock – the Manipulators try to sneak prices up as high as they can without anyone noticing because they know that once prices start to take-off, everyone is going to notice it and want to get a piece of the action. If the majority of the public notices too early on, gets excited and gets in then they would be entering the market much closer to the bottom. The rally would then reach its top at a much lower price range, lose steam and fall. There would be no buyers left to take it to higher prices, so it would have no other choice but to fall when the selling pressure starts (or should I say when Manipulator support ends).

The Manipulators know that the sooner everyone gets in, the sooner it reaches its high. So, in order for prices to go as high as possible before cashing out, they want to make the take-off point as high as possible – just like our base runner who wants his take-off point (the point where he starts to run) as far as possible from first base to increase his likelihood of getting to second base safely.

This is what the markup phase is all about – the sneaking up portion "before" the runner starts to run.

(Chart courtesy of Prophet.Net)

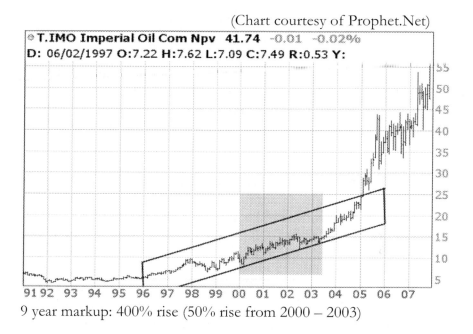

T.IMO Imperial Oil Com Npv 41.74 -0.01 -0.02%
D: 06/02/1997 O:7.22 H:7.62 L:7.09 C:7.49 R:0.53 Y:

9 year markup: 400% rise (50% rise from 2000 – 2003)

Notice how Imperial Oil made its way to new highs in 1996 finally breaking above the $5.00 barrier which had stood for 4 years. Prices then proceeded to sneak their way slowly and quietly from $5.00 to $25 over the course of the next 9 years. A 400% rise may seem like a big move that most people would get excited about, however, you have to put this into perspective with respect to the time frame involved. A $20 rise in price over 9 years is the same as this stock moving upwards (on average) 1 cent per trading day. Thinking about it in those terms, you can see how the Manipulators are able to sneak prices higher without you even noticing.

Prices rallied and fell back, rallied and fell back, rallied and fell back again, all the while creeping their way to new highs each time. This is the kind of price action that causes most investors to lose their patience, lose their faith, and sell. This is the kind of price action that causes investors to sit on the sidelines watching because prices appear weak, unable to make any significant progress, falling back time and time again. This is the kind of price action that allows the Manipulators to sneak their way out from first base, as they prepare to steal second.

How many times have you looked at a stock, noticed that it wasn't really going anywhere fast and you kind of just turned your attention elsewhere. But, when you did come back to check on it weeks or months or even years later you noticed that it had crept up very slowly (day by day) but overall it was quite a bit higher than when you first looked at it. You thought to yourself – "oh boy, if I would have just got in when I first looked at it, I would be up some nice profits by now".

Well, why didn't you? Because of bad luck. No, because of manipulation. The Manipulators know that this type of price movement is not encouraging. The average investor does not have the patience to wait out a long, slow, steady upward move, even if it's happening right before their eyes. The public sees prices moving slowly, setting back once in a while and interprets this action as a stock that is having trouble going up, therefore it must be weak. They conclude that it will not likely go much higher so there's no point in buying it. Or, if they are already a shareholder, they see a slow rise in prices followed by a setback and once again conclude that the stock is weak, therefore, they had better get out before it falls further. This is Manipulation at its finest. It's like staring at the minute hand on your watch. Even though you know it is moving, because you can't really see it move, you turn your attention away. And then, when you look back, it has actually moved quite a bit further than you would have thought.

(Chart courtesy of Prophet.Net)

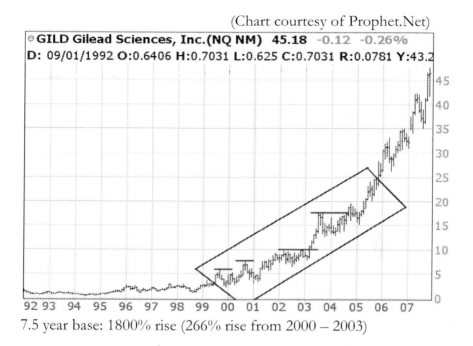

GILD Gilead Sciences, Inc.(NQ NM) 45.18 -0.12 -0.26%
D: 09/01/1992 O:0.6406 H:0.7031 L:0.625 C:0.7031 R:0.0781 Y:43.2

7.5 year base: 1800% rise (266% rise from 2000 – 2003)

Gilead Sciences is a great example of the slow steady price action that takes place during the markup phase. Notice how each time prices hit new highs they fell back. They then rallied again to new highs and fell back, rallied again, bumped into a false ceiling, and then traded sideways for 1 or 2 years.

Remember, the Manipulator's goal is to sneak prices as high as they can, while at the same time drawing as little attention to the "rise" as possible. The more of the public they can keep out of the market, the more control they will retain and ultimately the higher they will be able to drive prices before selling in the top range. They are literally sneaking their way out from first base – getting as close to second base as they can before they start to run. This will give them the greatest chance of success when they attempt to steal second or in our case, steal millions of dollars from the uninformed, unsuspecting public.

THEY know that the public desires speed, needs speed. THEY know the public is trying to make the most money possible in the least amount of time. Well, what's wrong with that? The Law of Cause and

Effect – that's what. You are trying to defy one of the Natural Laws of the Universe.

"Less in" does not equate to "more out."

Yes, of course there are situations where everything will work out just right and you will make some big profits in a very short period of time. But, by and large, you will earn (if you have the patience and drive to study and practice), the vast majority of your profits over the course of months and years not days.

The Manipulators know that they can keep you out as long as they keep prices moving quietly because it goes against your nature to see this action and think to yourself, "WOW! If I get in now and wait this out for months, or even years, I could make some really nice profits way down the road". No – you say to yourself, "this stock looks weak, like it's having trouble going up, and since it is just barely making new highs each day, it probably won't be able to go much higher". You have just been caught in THEIR trap. THEY are sneaking, (inching) their way towards second base and you're the pitcher standing on the mound with your back turned.

(Chart courtesy of Prophet.Net)

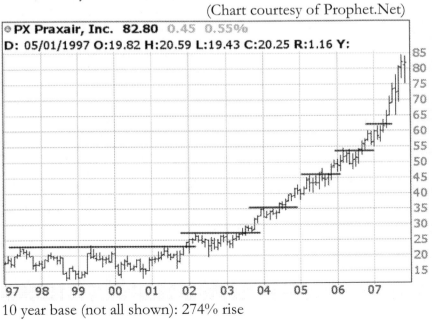

10 year base (not all shown): 274% rise

What happens next is no surprise. Prices continue to gain momentum and move higher all the while the public sit on the sidelines watching and trading other stocks that are exhibiting violent swings in price, and showing huge daily volumes. This is what the public gets excited about. This is where they think they can make some fast, easy money. Did you ever think about how and why day trading became so popular and widespread in 1999 and 2000? Why so many people sitting at home in front of their computers felt that they could all of a sudden open an account with a broker, maybe subscribe to a real time streaming data service, and start to trade and make money consistently with no experience or knowledge whatsoever? The answer is, to use THEIR terminology, <u>one of the biggest bull markets in history</u>, that's what. There's an old saying:

"Don't mistake a BULL MARKET for brains."

Unfortunately, most investors did. Everybody knew someone who was trading at home and making money. It was easy. Do a little research, read a few news articles, get a tip from a friend (also who didn't have any experience) and that was it. Place an order and watch as prices climbed higher and higher. It was quick, easy money. Who could resist?

Few people, if any, actually realized that is was not them, and their "brains" that allowed them to succeed, but rather a period of time in which most of the well known, big name stocks were all experiencing markup at the same time. You could have closed your eyes and thrown a dart at the stock page and made money in 1999. But most people figured that they had somehow figured it all out, and were patting themselves on the back for their stock picking prowess.

Unfortunately, these people did realize it, but way too late. These were the same people who rode those profits all the way back down to the bottom again when the inevitable markdown phase eroded away as much as 90% of their stock's value. Had they really been smart, they would have sold out at the top, and realized their profits like the Manipulators. Instead they joined the masses (buying high and selling low) because they were NOT, in fact, investing with their brains, but rather with their emotions.

This same philosophy or attitude holds true throughout all of the phases of the price cycle. Most of the public sees the slow creeping up action of markup and they turn their attention elsewhere because they don't believe they can make money fast enough or even at all because of the tired, weak looking action.

Again, the Manipulators are slowly allowing prices to creep higher and, the public is off losing money in the top range somewhere else because somewhere, there's a stock that's presumably showing some real promise – trapped again. This is what you have to condition yourself against. You have to learn to be a contrarian. Think contrary to the masses and you will come out on top. Follow the masses and you will be swallowed up by the Manipulators time and time again.

If the best 3 words to describe accumulation are:

- **quiet**
- **sideways**
- **discouraging**

then the best 3 words to describe markup would be:

- **setbacks**
- **consolidations**
- **sneaking-up**

Consolidation refers to price activity that moves in a mostly sideways manner becoming squeezed into a narrower range.

(Chart courtesy of Prophet.Net)

CRRC Courier Corporation(NQ NM) 14.76 -0.56 -3.66%
D: 07/01/1986 O:0.9976 H:0.9976 L:0.9004 C:0.9137 R:0.0972 Y:

85   87 88 89 90 91 92 93 94 95 96 97 98 99 00 01 02 03 04 05 06 07

13 year base: 1600% rise (300% rise from 2000 – 2003)

Notice the 13 year accumulation base of Courier Corp. from 1985 – 1997. This is your signal - this is your treasure map – this is the foundation for a high rise not a mere rally. Look at how prices slowly crept their way from $2.50 to $27.50 over the course of 7 years. Would you have entered this market? Would you have then had the faith and patience to hang on each time prices stalled and fell back during the early stages of mark-up? With knowledge of the man-made price cycle, and a 13 year base behind you, your answer should be YES to both questions.

How do they do it? How do they keep the majority of the public on the sidelines as prices move higher and higher, in spite of the fact that most of the public view a worthy investment as a stock that is already moving? How are the Manipulators able to move prices to much higher levels without causing too much excitement amongst investors? By sneaking their way up, by taking their time, by dragging it out with setbacks and consolidations. Let's take a closer look at Courier Corporation and zoom in on the markup phase itself.

(Chart courtesy of Prophet.Net)

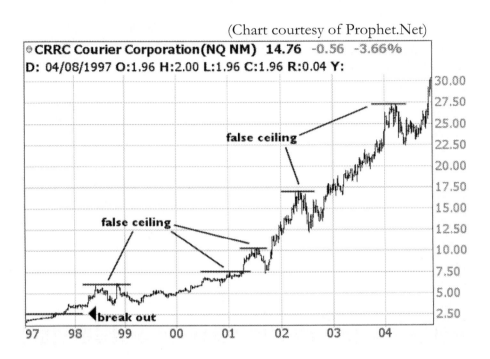

During markup, the Manipulators #1 weapon is sneaking tactics. Just when you think prices are ready to go higher, they hit a false ceiling stall, and setback. Just when you think prices are ready to rally again, they hit another ceiling and trade sideways for weeks or months or even years. The Manipulators lull you into believing that because prices are moving slowly, they must be weak, therefore stay away or get out if you're already in.

What do WE all want - we, meaning the investing public? Once prices start moving up, we want them to keep going, we want them to increase the speed of their rise, and we want them to never look back. But markup is nothing like that. Markup is all about sneaking up. Its about two steps forward one step back, three steps forward two steps back, two steps forward, three steps back. And, this process is happening over the course of months and years, not days or weeks as most of us would prefer.

This kind of price action is not happening by chance. Advancing prices are purposefully held in check, held back, to test your patience, or more specifically to wear out your patience. This is why so many investors end up on the sidelines despite the fact that prices are doing exactly what they had hoped for, moving higher and higher. In their greed and impatience, the public not only requires prices to advance, but they also require them to advance quickly. This tendency for speed is the investor's undoing. That, and being unaware of the price cycle itself - unaware of why prices move the way they do. And why, when they finally do get underway, they move slowly, one step at a time, often times falling back or trading in a sideways pattern for many months or years.

Just as patience is required to wait for the accumulation phase to complete before entering a market, so too is patience required during markup while you're watching your profits slowly increase, decrease and then increase again. Prices that slowly creep higher and higher, tend go unnoticed by the majority of the public because the public only has faith in stocks that are showing "what they believe to be" strength (i.e., large volumes, big daily price swings, prices that are advancing quickly, stocks that are reported on regularly in the news). If fact, you can see now that the exact opposite is the case.

Think of it in terms of constructing a tower on which to erect a diving board. If laying the concrete foundation for our tower could be likened to that of the accumulation phase when prices are building their base, then the construction of the tower, one rung at a time, higher and higher, would be similar to our slow and methodical rise in prices during the markup phase.

- The more rungs that are added, the higher the platform.

- The higher the platform, the higher the diving board is from the water.

- The higher the diving board is from the water, the higher the takeoff point from where the diver springs upwards reaching his highest level (distribution) before falling all the way back down to the water (markdown).

And of course, what happens just before the diver springs up to his highest level? He actually loses height from his takeoff point as he drives the diving board downward absorbing his weight, building up pressure for his launch to higher levels. This is just like stocks, which usually have one last major setback prior to speeding upwards to their ultimate highs (as seen here in 2004 on the chart of Pulte Homes).

(Chart courtesy of Prophet.Net)

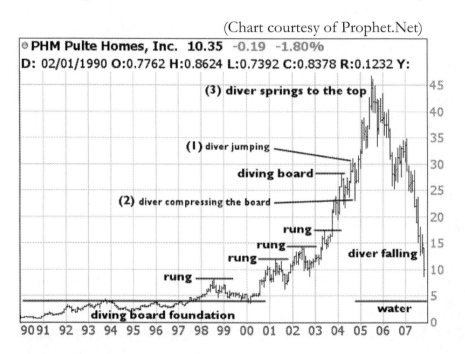

1975 – 1997 (not all shown)
Accumulation Base = foundation for our diving tower

1997 – 2004
Markup Phase = building of the tower, one rung at a time

2004 – 2006
Distribution = diver launching his way to his highest point

2006 – 2007
Markdown Phase = diver falling all the way back down to the water

Notice how it took 6.5 years for prices to move from $5.00 to $25 during accumulation and markup, but it only took them one year to advance from $25 to $45 during distribution. This is the greatest distinction between markup and distribution — the rate of speed at which prices rise.

And ultimately, as with gravity, that which goes up must come down. Prices are making their way back down to the $5.00 level from where they started. Had this tower for Pulte not been built as high, had the Manipulators not taken the time to slowly but surely add more and more rungs during markup, then when it came time for the diver to spring upwards, he would have never made it to the same high level before falling back to the water.

What this means to the Manipulators is being able to unload the majority of their shares at a much higher level, resulting in greater profits for them (and for you, now that you are aware of their practice).

Remember that all price cycles will take different forms and run on their own time line, but in the end, the concept of sneaking prices higher and higher ultimately results in a greater percentage rise off the bottom.

So,

- knowing that a large accumulation base of many years in the bottom range preceding markup is the foundation for a high rise, not a mere rally, and,

- knowing that markup is a slow, gradual process comprised of a series of setbacks, consolidations, and sneaking prices, and,

- knowing that distribution is the inevitable result of markup because the Manipulators require wild, exciting price action in the top range to lure the public into buying from them (those shares they need to unload to reap their reward),

- you, as a Price Cycle savvy investor, with lots of study and practice can gain the kind of patience and faith which will allow you to identify periods of accumulation, enter on breakouts, and then ride out the inescapable ups and downs of early markup en-route to much higher prices.

In order for Distribution to occur at high prices, markup needs to be slow, so have faith that it is taking time for a reason. The Manipulators are trying to erect as tall a tower as they can before springing their way to the ultimate top.

Now, let's have a look at how they are able to sneak prices higher and higher right under our noses.

False Support

Often, prices will come to a screeching halt before they ever really get going. Lines of support appear all over your charts but when a line of support appears too perfect, too strong, that's a good time to be suspicious, as in the case with Ryland Group (next page). After prices broke out of their base in mid 1997, they proceeded to trade in a mostly sideways manner for 2 years exhibiting a strong line of support at approx. $4.50. Through all of 1998 and 1999 public shareholders felt good about the fact that even though prices weren't rising in their favour yet, at least they were well supported and unable to fall below $4.50. Well, whenever a support (or resistance level for that matter) appears too perfect, chances are it isn't, and eventually will be broken. Prices did break through to the downside and made their way to $3.50 very quickly. This drop in prices would have surely had the desired effect with shareholders running for the exits. Not coincidentally, this drop in prices came at the exact time the DOW and NASDAQ began their prolonged fall from all time highs.

(Chart courtesy of Prophet.Net)

RYL Ryland Group, Inc. 21.38 0.24 1.14%
D: 04/07/1997 O:2.37 H:2.62 L:2.30 C:2.42 R:0.32 Y:

Remember when we talked about how the Manipulators are able to control prices. For two years (1998 and 1999) they supported prices with large buy orders on the bid side of the order desk such that each time prices fell back to $4.50, they were unable to go lower because the Manipulators would buy up more shares than were being offered for sale. Well what happened? After brainwashing the public into believing that prices couldn't fall below this level, they simply removed their buy orders and allowed prices to freefall to $3.50 where they then stepped in and lent support again. The public sold, the Manipulators bought on the way down, and six months later prices were right back above $5.00, but this time with far fewer public shareholders along for the ride.

Now, let's have a look at the big picture for Ryland Group.

(Chart courtesy of Prophet.Net)

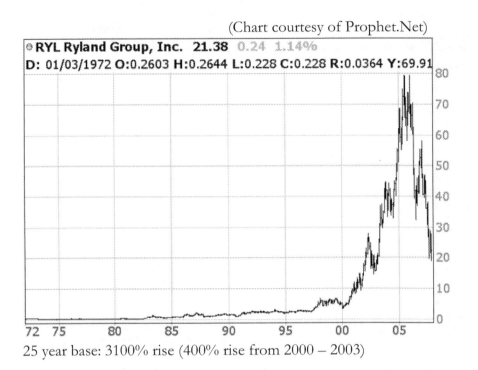

◈ RYL Ryland Group, Inc. 21.38 0.24 1.14%
D: 01/03/1972 O:0.2603 H:0.2644 L:0.228 C:0.228 R:0.0364 Y:69.91

25 year base: 3100% rise (400% rise from 2000 – 2003)

Now of course, the drop in price below the false support level in early 2000 turned out to be a final shakeout as prices rallied and never looked back again, until reaching their highs near $80 in 2005. This is a perfect example of price Manipulation. Prices were near their all time lows, but rather than buying down here at the bottom, the public was selling. This is what markup is all about and why it works so well. Being a Manipulator savvy investor, however, you wouldn't have fallen for this old trick. You would have either held through the setback, knowing you had a solid base behind you, or if you were not yet a shareholder, then you'd be waiting and watching for prices to recover and break back above false support prior to entering.

(Chart courtesy of Prophet.Net)

Whenever a support level appears too perfect, it's time to err on the side of caution. And, the longer this type of price movement goes on, the more suspicious you should become. Prices will usually tend to break in the direction of the flat top (or bottom), however, for Immucor, that was not the case as prices first broke out to the upside as seen here in 1999. With that said, sometimes, it is wiser to allow a breakout to the upside to get away, rather than to be caught in a false start of what is really a troubled formation in disguise.

Had you not entered on the breakout of the downtrending base in 1999, you would have still been following Immucor's price action and later realized that the drop below the false support level (which didn't come until 2000) was in fact a final shakeout in progress. From there, it was just a matter of watching and waiting for prices to recover before entering. Now here's the big picture for Immucor.

(Chart courtesy of Prophet.Net)

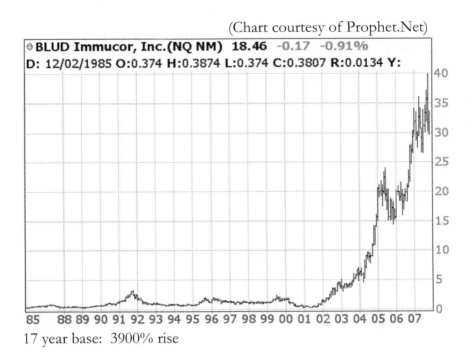

BLUD Immucor, Inc.(NQ NM) 18.46 -0.17 -0.91%
D: 12/02/1985 O:0.374 H:0.3874 L:0.374 C:0.3807 R:0.0134 Y:

17 year base: 3900% rise

Keep on the lookout for false support levels in all phases of the price cycle.

You will see them used during **accumulation** as a method for the Manipulators to increase the size of their position in the bottom range.

You will see them used during **markup** as a means for the Manipulators to sneak prices higher without exciting the public into the market too early.

You will see them used during **distribution** as a way for the Manipulators to keep prices appearing strong in order to draw public buyers in, allowing them an opportunity to unload their shares in the top range.

And, you will see them used during **markdown** as a technique to induce the public back in - in search of a bargain. But, which results in an opportunity for the Manipulators to sell off the last of their shares into false rallies during a falling market.

False Ceilings

Whenever it appears as though prices have hit an impenetrable boundary and can't go any higher, that's a good sign that they eventually will. This is one of the Manipulator's most widely used strategies to trick you into making wrong decisions.

A false ceiling is a resistance level that prices bump up against many times, usually over the course of many months or years, acting as if they cannot go any higher. The reason it is called a "false" ceiling is because in most cases, prices eventually do go higher. For the Manipulator savvy investor, this is one of the best signals we can hope to find on our long term charts both in terms of offering us definite entry points, as well as, bolstering our confidence in the continuation of the markup phase to higher prices. The false ceiling acts as both its own price formation as well as a type of discouraging price activity that when incorporated into other price patterns (channels, flat top triangles, and head & shoulder formations), makes them all the more effective.

Sometimes these formations will take the shape of a triangle with a flat top, while other times they just look like a channel with an undefined bottom boundary. In either case, they produce the desired effect every time they are used. Whenever you spot a multi-year price consolidation with a flat top in the bottom range, you had better be ready to act.

(Chart courtesy of Prophet.Net)

5 year base: 1525% rise

AmeriCredit Corp. shows us a picture perfect example of the man-made price cycle in action and how it incorporates many of the price controlling actions that we have discussed so far. The accumulation phase is made up of extremely low volume, sideways, discouraging price action in the bottom range over many years. The markup phase starts out with a breakout above the $4.00 false ceiling in 1995. This is where you would have entered had you been watching at that time. Prices slowly crept their way up for 3 years before running into another ceiling of resistance at $19. After 2.5 years of weak looking prices, investors started to trust that prices couldn't go any higher. Of course they did, because that is the very purpose of consolidation, a rest before the rise. When prices broke through their false ceiling at $19, you would have entered there had you been watching at that time. Notice the sharp final shakeout (FSO) from $19 down to $10 in early 2000 immediately preceding the rally. Isn't it amazing how prices can apparently be so weak just prior to being so very strong?

(Chart courtesy of Prophet.Net)

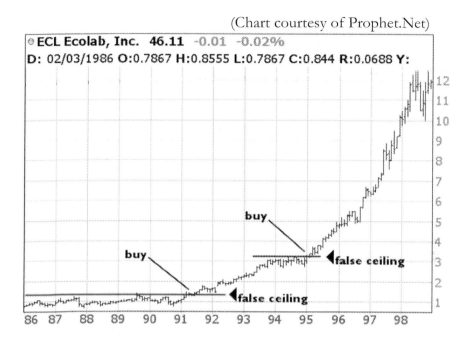

ECL Ecolab, Inc. **46.11** -0.01 -0.02%
D: 02/03/1986 O:0.7867 H:0.8555 L:0.7867 C:0.844 R:0.0688 Y:

When looking at charts like Ecolab, always remember the big picture. And, always remember what prices are attempting to do during markup – to sneak their way hundreds of percent higher over time without drawing too much attention. The way they do this is to follow up every rally with either a setback or consolidation, or both. Every time prices advance they are quickly reined in and allowed to rest prior to the next rally. It would be like containing and conserving the pent up energy of a bucking bronco after releasing him from his stall. Rather than letting the horse's energy disperse all at once in 30 seconds of continuous bucking, the handlers would allow the bronco to only buck for 10 seconds, after which they would corral the horse back into his stall and allow him to rest prior to his next release.

Then they would repeat this process a number of times stretching out the horse's bucking ability over a longer period of time. This is how the energy of prices is contained and conserved, resulting in a higher top than would otherwise be achieved if prices were left to advance without setback or consolidation. The trade off, however, is that this process requires much more time. Now, here's the big picture for Ecolab.

(Chart courtesy of Prophet.Net)

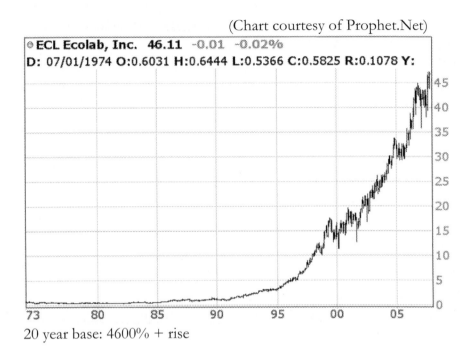

20 year base: 4600% + rise

The problem is that most people tend to interpret time as a negative, meaning the longer it takes for a stock to rise, the weaker it is. Unfortunately, this backwards perception of price movement leads them to sell - when the biggest part of the move is still to come. This is why we buy on the breakout and not before. Trying to guess at an entry point will in most cases have you buying in the middle of a formation which means you will most likely have to ride out losses for months or years, waiting for the next big move to begin. Your patience will fade and you will be caught selling, (most likely during a final shakeout) just before prices rally to new highs.

Again, referring to Ecolab, (being a Manipulator savvy investor) you would have not only bought on the breakout of the 5 year false ceiling in 1991, but again when prices broke above their 1.5 year false ceiling in January 1995. By buying on the breakout you would have put the majority of the waiting time behind you, and then, any waiting you would have done, would have been with profits. This is a much easier way to maintain your faith, as opposed to holding losses for years waiting for a formation to play itself out.

Head & Shoulders Formations

In an earlier section, we looked at how the Manipulators use the head and shoulders formation during the accumulation base as a means of inducing the public to sell in the bottom range. Now we will explore how they use it during markup as a sneaking-up tactic.

During markup, and with prices slowly on the rise, discouraging price patterns are used to: (i) induce profit taking by those few, fortunate investors who actually did buy at the bottom and (ii) to discourage buying by those who are watching from the sidelines. The head and shoulders formation accomplishes both of these goals.

Any situation during markup that causes the public to sell and/or to lose interest and turn their buying attention elsewhere results in a further building-up of internal strength. This build-up is very similar to what would happen to a mountain climber attempting an ambitious ascent up a mountain. There is a not a climber that I am aware of who can climb, without rest or delay, from base to summit in one continuous stretch. Climbers tire along the way and require rest periods every so often to re-energize themselves prior to pushing higher. If a climber were to attempt to make it to the summit in one continuous push, his body would eventually give way, no matter how fit he was, and he would fall far short of his target.

Such is the case with price action during the markup phase. Prices require delays and rest periods if they ever hope to make it to their ultimate top. Sometimes the delays and rest periods will be longer, sometimes shorter, but they are nonetheless always present.

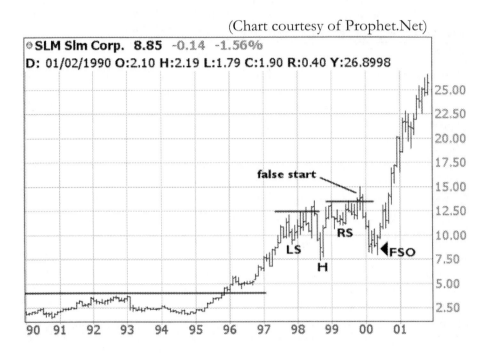

(Chart courtesy of Prophet.Net)

As you know, the way in which a mountain climber re-energizes and prepares himself for another push up the mountain is to get some sleep, rest his body, take in some much needed nutrients and prepare his supplies for the next stage of the climb. Similarly, when prices appear tired and weak, they too are re-energizing themselves for another push up the price mountain.

Referring to SLM Corp., the net result of this price action is for the Manipulators to gain back some of the control which they have been gradually letting go of as a result of selling their shares to interested investors along the path from $3.75 (the breakout level of the accumulation base) to $12.50 (the false ceiling of the left shoulder). Once prices reached $12.50, the Manipulators decided that it was time to discourage and frighten some of those investors right back out of the market.

By directing prices to trade in a depressing manner for 3 years (head and shoulders formation), they were able to buy back those same shares they sold on the way up. This allowed them to once again increase the size of their holding and regain more control in preparation for another push up the price mountain.

Just as the first 233% rise ($3.75 to $12.50) was facilitated by the control they gained during accumulation, the Manipulators needed to re-acquire some of the control they lost on the way up. The false ceilings and violent setbacks of the head and shoulders formation did just that. The public sold and/or were discouraged from buying and the Manipulators grew stronger for another push on their way to the summit.

You may have thought that the head and shoulders formation would have been enough to divert attention away from this stock, however, the Manipulators still had one more trick up their sleeves. Obviously, there were still investors who were hanging on as well as investors who spotted the opportunity in SLM Corp. to buy on the breakout of the right shoulder. So what did the Manipulators do? They turned the breakout of the right shoulder into a false start.

These moves are meant to trick even the savviest investor into believing that prices are on the rise again. As a result, investors enter the market, but are then quickly disappointed, getting right back out with a loss when prices fall back below their entry point. And many times, the setback following a false start turns out to be violent in nature, resulting in what's known as a final shakeout (as seen with SLM Corp. in 2000).

First prices are allowed to rise to $15 in 1999 to trick investors to buy, and then that rise is quickly followed up with a severe, final shakeout all the way down back down to $8.00 in 2000. Not many investors would have been able to hold through this drop in prices.

This action illustrates yet another example of how prices can act so very weak just prior to becoming so very strong. From the final shakeout in 2000, prices never looked back as they continued with their markup, and then on into distribution on their way to all time highs near $60 (next page). That's why I'm sure, you, along with the rest of us have at one time or another uttered those famous words, **"as soon as I sold, it took off."** This is yet more evidence that the

Manipulators are able to alter perspective and trick you and the rest of the public into selling, when in fact you should be buying or holding.

(Chart courtesy of Prophet.Net)

13 year base: 1400% rise (300% rise from 2000 – 2003)

The false start/final shakeout scenario in boxing terms is the Manipulators' one-two punch. They hit you high, you enter the market, then they hit you low, and you exit with a loss. When they go high again, rather than entering the market, you duck out of the way, passing on the opportunity to re-enter for fear that the low blow is next. Of course it doesn't come, prices continue to move higher and you're left on the sidelines with a loss, watching as prices double over the course of the next year.

It can be nerve racking to hold through these final shakeouts but the trade off is not much more appealing. That would be to sell before prices drop too far and then try to re-enter during the setback. This is not an easy proposition and one that would, if repeated too many times, lull you right back into your old, short term market perspective of trying to call perfectly, every up and down of prices. In the long run, you will fair much better by holding with confidence through these shakeouts. **But, only when they occur in the very earliest stages of markup after prices have recently broke up and out of a long period of consolidation.**

Consolidations

Consolidations are situations where prices trade in a range defined by easily identifiable boundaries. The two most common boundaries appearing on your long term charts are channels and triangles. You will also see shapes known as wedges, however, we will consider them part of the channel family since they resemble channels (except they tend to be turned up on a bit of an angle, and sometimes have one end that's narrower than the other).

The purpose of consolidation is to make prices appear tired and out of steam when, in fact, the exact opposite is the case. These consolidations will occur most frequently during markup because this is the phase where the Manipulators need to move prices slowly over time without arousing too much public interest. Having prices trade in a confined pattern for months or years is an ideal way to accomplish this.

The result of this price action is a building-up of internal strength as the public loses patience and sells or sits on the sidelines watching and waiting for more exciting action. Sooner or later this bottled up strength will burst through its boundary and proceed to higher ground. That result is a signal for us to enter the market if we're not already in or to add to our position if we already are. It also gives us further evidence and confirmation that prices are proceeding on their unalterable course from accumulation to markup to distribution.

After prices break out of a large accumulation base and rally to the upside, the public starts to notice. Since the Manipulators are trying to avoid attention, they need to do divert the public's new found interest. What better way than to have prices trade in an increasingly boring, sideways manner over a long period of time. Pretty soon the public begins to believe that prices are weak and aren't going any higher. If they're in, they're patience grows thin and they get out, and turn their attention to other stocks that are exhibiting more promising action (probably stocks in distribution). The longer prices consolidate, the more and more the stock in question drops off of everyone's radar — until the next rally of course.

• Channels

(Chart courtesy of Prophet.Net)

8 yr base & 9 yrs of consolidation: 2750% rise to $57 in 2006 (not all shown)

The price action for Thor Industries shows us three periods of consolidation. The first, in the form of an accumulation base, which is followed up by two channels (B) and (C). Just as a long period of accumulation is the building-up of a solid foundation (on which to support a high rise), periods of consolidation during early markup add yet another level of support and strength from which to push prices even higher. More consolidation means more internal strength. And more strength, means a greater rise for prices. Not only do these formations give us a key as to how high prices will eventually go, but they also provide us with opportunities as to when to enter a market. You have heard me talk about entering the market on breakouts rather than trying to pick a bottom. The reason being that not only are we attempting to make profits but we are also attempting to limit our waiting time as best we can (based on what the price cycle is willing to offer us).

Even though we don't have any control over the markup phase and how long it will take to reach distribution, we do have control over the period of time we choose to be invested. Therefore, we need to choose carefully as to when to be in, and when to be out, to have the maximum return on both our invested dollars and our time.

Opportunity cost is defined as "the cost of a lost opportunity due to a foregone alternative". This simply means that if you tie up your money in an investment that is going sideways, that money is not otherwise available to be invested in another stock that's moving higher and producing a greater return. Therefore, what is the cost of that lost opportunity?

STOCK MARKET MYTH #4
Short, Medium or Long Term Investing

How do you categorize your investment approach? Do you buy and sell stocks over the course of days, weeks and months. Is your holding time in the 1 - 2 year time frame? Or do you hold even longer, 3 – 5 years?

Since we do know that stock prices move based on their individual price cycle. And, since we don't know how long each individual markup phase will last, **HOW CAN YOU** or **WHY WOULD YOU** decide in advance what your investment holding period will be?

To arbitrarily say that you are a long term investor (and that means holding any stocks that you buy for at least 5 years) would be like saying that because Tiger Woods is a long ball hitter, he's going to decide at the beginning of the golf season to tee off using his driver on every par 4 and par 5 hole on every course that he plays for that entire season. As you can imagine, this pre-determined strategy would likely work extremely well on some holes, but be disastrous on others. Just as holding stocks for 5 years would be extremely profitable in some cases, but produce significant losses in others.

Instead, what does Tiger do? He reacts to each situation as it is presented and adjusts his hitting strategy to short, medium or long based on what will allow him to reach his target in the safest, most efficient manner. Just as students of the price cycle need to adjust their holding strategy based on what is being presented to them on each individual price chart that they follow.

When volatile, choppy price action rears its head during markup and/or on into distribution, it's time to be looking for an opportunity to sell, whether you've been holding for 8 days, 8 weeks, 8 months or 8 years. It's time to start referring to yourself as a "profitable" investor and react to what is being offered to you on your long term price charts.

If you invest in XYZ stock and it reaches distribution in 6 months and then begins markdown, a pre-set long term investing strategy will do you no good in this scenario. Likewise, if you invest in ABC stock, watch it rise 20% in one month and then sell on the first setback; you may be cheating yourself out of hundreds of percent in profit if its markup phase carries on for the next 2 years.

Be patient, but be ready and take what each stock is willing to give. Sometimes you'll get shaken out early and other times you'll hold on a little too long. But in the grand scheme of things, if you can change your perspective to that of being a "profitable" investor, you'll be well on your way to making the most of your opportunities.

(Chart courtesy of Prophet.Net)

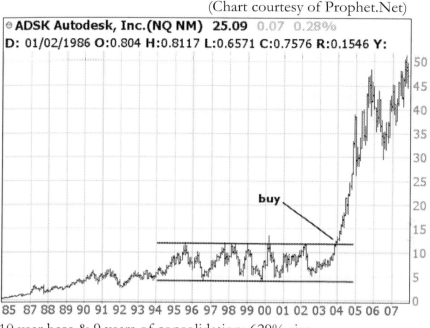

10 year base & 9 years of consolidation: 629% rise

Your greatest return on time to profit will almost always be during the period after prices breakout of a large formation as shown with Autodesk. Don't let greed get in your way by trying to pick bottoms. Sometimes those apparent bottoms will turn out to be either long periods of consolidation or downtrends in price, which may result in a long wait with heavy losses. It's always better to buy on the breakout and be in profits as soon as possible. This provides you with some cushion and a lot more peace of mind during your wait. Better to wait out a long markup holding profits than to wait out a setback or consolidation with a loss.

However, there are also situations where you will do everything right and it still turns out to be a long wait and that's OK. There is no way to know in advance if a markup is going to last 1 year or 10 years, that's why we spread our money around in hopes of catching a few of the faster ones - knowing that we will certainly get stuck waiting out some of the slower ones. This was certainly the case with Forest Labs (next page). Had you bought on the breakout of the accumulation base back in 1991 you would have had a long wait as prices consolidated for an additional seven years before proceeding to significantly higher highs.

(Chart courtesy of Prophet.Net)

21 year base & 7 years of consolidation: 1900% rise

Buying on the breakout at the beginning of the base in 1991 and then again on the breakout of the consolidation channel in early 1998 would have been all you could do to maximize your investment of time and money on this stock. But with that said, it still doesn't keep you from having to be patient along with the Manipulators while they proceed to slowly inch prices up over time, before finally allowing them to take off for the summit. You may have ended up holding this stock for the better part of 13 years, but the wait would have been well worth it. Prices eventually did make their way to the summit in the form of a 1900% rise off its base.

CAVEAT

Most of the charts we've looked at so far have demonstrated significant rises in price ranging anywhere from a couple hundred percent up to as much as 4000% or more. Please note that by showing you these examples, I am by no means trying to imply that you will be able to profit to this extent as it relates to your investing strategy. These charts are merely meant to show you the BIG PICTURE.

They are meant to show you the truth about what is happening to these stocks, and what will happen to the stocks you intend to trade in the future. In as much as it may be unrealistic to think that we can buy in at the very bottom and then sell out at the very top, it is not unrealistic to expect that we can buy on breakouts of large accumulation bases, hold on during the early setbacks and consolidation periods, add to our positions when given the appropriate signals and then sell part way through the markup phase. It is not unrealistic to expect to garner profits in the 100% - 500% range, as these price rises (in most cases) represent only a small portion of the overall markup phase.

Remember, we are not pre-determining a target for ourselves, nor are we able to know in advance how high each markup will go. We are simply following the price action that presents itself to us on our long term charts and then reacting to what we see. Every price mountain is different just as every mountain summit reaches up to a different height. That's why we have to make sure we don't have all of our investment eggs in one basket.

STOCK MARKET MYTH #5
Diversification Reduces Risk

Diversifying for the wrong reason may simply serve to complicate an already bad situation. If you're a poor stock picker, then all that diversifying will do is to turn one or two losses into four or five losses as you buy more stocks in hopes of spreading out your risk.

Chances are, whatever perception, emotions, and rationale caused you to pick those first couple of stocks, will invariably lead you to make more bad decisions when it comes to buying number three, four, and five.

With your new found knowledge of the man-made price cycle, however, **diversifying now becomes a means to maximize profits rather than to limit losses.**

Diversification is not about turning large losses into small losses, it's about increasing your opportunities to <u>realize</u> profits in a more timely fashion. Now that's not to say that you won't experience losses, everyone does. However, the point I'm trying to make is that the concept of diversification should bring about (FOR YOU) an altered perception - that being one of timely profits, as opposed to limited losses.

Let's say you're invested in one stock, but that stock is involved in a long, slow 10 year markup. Although that's a good thing, you haven't as yet realized any gain from it as you patiently hold, and watch as your profits slowly increase over time. What if, on the other hand, you were invested in 10 well accumulated stocks at the same time? Chances are some would reach distribution in 10 years, others in five years and still others in one or two years. And, as you have seen, as some stocks produce 100 – 200% returns, others will reach upwards of 500 - 1000% or more. By owning a basket of well accumulated stocks, you are effectively diversifying your opportunity to enjoy some of those quicker markup phases, and increasing your chances of hitting one of those larger rises, rather than having all your eggs tied up in one basket, so to speak. Because, if that one basket turns out to be a 10 year markup and a mere 100% rise off the base, you will certainly not be capitalizing on your all of your opportunities.

Remember there are only three things that we do not know (in advance),

(1) When a stock will begin markup,

(2) how long it will take to reach distribution and,

(3) how high it will ultimately go.

Therefore, diversify yourself into a number of well accumulated stocks and let the Manipulators take it from there.

You may have noticed (after looking at all these examples) and be asking yourself, "if we are trying to maximize our time to profit, then why don't we invest in the second half of markup rather than the first half? The second half shows that prices consistently move much higher, and much faster." The reason is that the second half of markup is more volatile than the first half. It is much harder to hold on through the 25% - 50% setbacks which occur more frequently during this stage of the price cycle. Invariably, this emotional roller coaster ride of watching your profits increase and then evaporate just as quickly will push the emotional element of your decision making process to the forefront, leading you back to a "pack" mentality and away from profits.

(Chart courtesy of Prophet.Net)

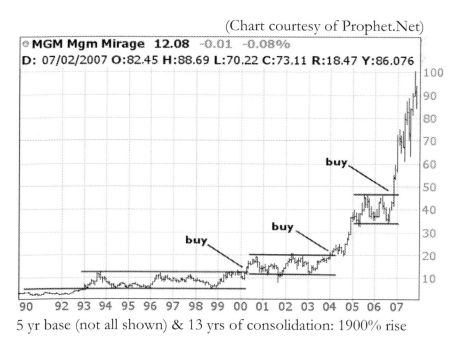

5 yr base (not all shown) & 13 yrs of consolidation: 1900% rise

With MGM Mirage (previous page), a great deal of internal pressure was built-up during the base and subsequent 7 years of consolidation from 1993 – 1999. Some of that pressure, however, was released during the 100% rise is prices from $10 - $20. In this example, prices required another building-up of pressure before another significant rise would be able to take place. And that's exactly what happened with the 4 year consolidation from 2000 - 2003. Prices then rose again from $20 - $45 all the while releasing some of that new found internal strength. Prices required one more consolidation before having the strength to push through to their summit.

A good way to relate to this concept is to think of it in terms of blowing up balloons. With each breath, more and more air is forced into the balloon. The longer you blow, the larger the balloon becomes, and the greater the pressure that is being built-up inside. If you were to let the balloon go after having only blown into it a few times, it wouldn't fly very far or for very long because the pressure built-up inside wouldn't have been that great.

On the other hand, if you were to let that same balloon go after having blown into it for a long period of time, the pressure built-up inside would be so great as to send that balloon flying around the room for some time after being released. This is what consolidation periods are like. The longer and more compact the consolidation, the greater the internal pressure that is being built-up, and in most cases, the greater the rise that can be expected when prices are finally released.

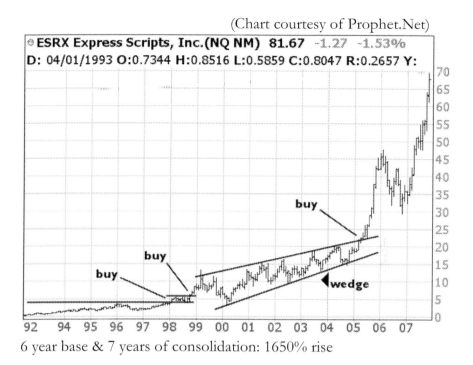

(Chart courtesy of Prophet.Net)

6 year base & 7 years of consolidation: 1650% rise

Express Scripts is a good example of how channels can sometimes form what are referred to as wedges. The period of consolidation from 1999 to 2004 reveals a channel propped up on a bit of an angle. Even though it isn't flat like the other channels we've seen, it does have all the same properties and produces the same results. Remember, the Manipulators will do anything and everything to get you out of the market at the bottom or to keep you from getting in, so if this is the type of price action that will work for them, then that's what they'll use.

After a solid 6 year base followed by a tight one year consolidation in 1998, the 6 year channeling consolidation (wedge) added a significant amount of internal pressure to this stock. And, of course, with more pressure comes more pop.

• Triangles

(Chart courtesy of Prophet.Net)

FDO Family Dollar Stores, Inc. 28.68 0.48 1.70%
D: 06/02/1975 O:0.0406 H:0.0659 L:0.039 C:0.0611 R:0.0268 Y:38.7

11 year base & 14 years of consolidation: 2500% rise

Just like Thor Industries (page 106), Family Dollar Stores exhibits two long consolidation periods after breaking out from its base. However, in this example, these consolidations take the shape of triangles rather than channels. Even though they form a different price pattern, the "WHY OF PRICES" remains the same. These consolidations are meant to trick the public into losing interest and turn their attention away. Just as with channels, buying on the breakout of the formation is always the recommended strategy in order to put you into the most profits in the least amount of time.

You will never know in advance whether the Manipulators will choose to use one, two or even three consolidation periods. Sometimes they may choose to forgo them altogether. That's why we put the odds in our favour as best we can by searching out sound stocks that not only have long accumulation bases, but also have one or more consolidation periods in early markup.

(Chart courtesy of Prophet.Net)

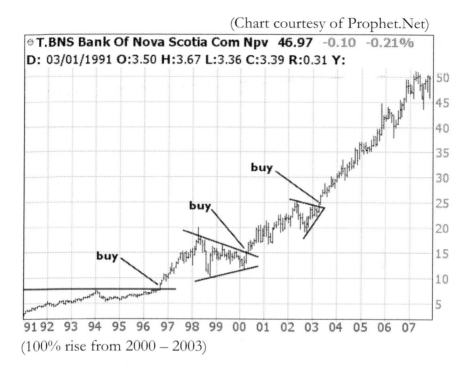

(100% rise from 2000 – 2003)

After a long channeling accumulation base of 24 years from 1973 - 1996 (not all shown), prices for Bank of Nova Scotia finally broke out to the upside in mid 1996 at the $7.50 level. You may have been tempted to sell when prices ran up quickly to approximately $20 in the next two years. However, you would certainly had been justified in holding through this setback knowing that a base of 23 years will almost always produce a much larger rise than a mere 166% ($7.50 to $20). Knowing the strength of the base behind you (had you sold during this first setback), you should certainly have been watching for your next entry point (again confident that an accumulation base of this magnitude is the foundation for a high rise not a mere rally). That next signal came in early 2000 at approximately $16 (coincidently right when "their" big Bear market started). Prices then continued higher with a slow, steady markup rising as much as 600% off its base.

(Chart courtesy of Prophet.Net)

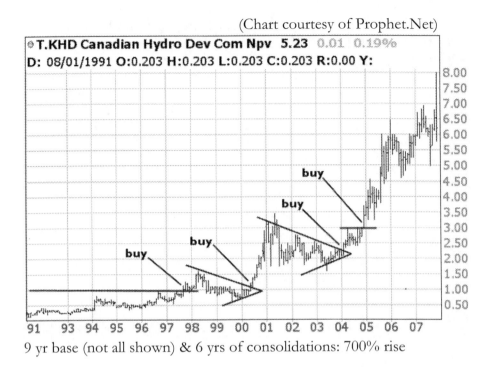

T.KHD Canadian Hydro Dev Com Npv 5.23 0.01 0.19%
D: 08/01/1991 O:0.203 H:0.203 L:0.203 C:0.203 R:0.00 Y:

9 yr base (not all shown) & 6 yrs of consolidations: 700% rise

Here's a good example of why I <u>don't</u> recommend using stop-sell orders after entering a sound stock on the breakout of a long base. Canadian Hydro Developers set up a 9 year accumulation base under $1.00. The breakout above $1.00 in late 1997 presented an excellent entry point. Had you also entered a stop-sell order at perhaps $0.90 (or even $0.80) to protect yourself against any subsequent setback, you would surely have been disappointed when prices fell back below your entry point in late 1998. Had you been alert enough to raise your stop as prices rose from $1.00 to approx. $1.50, you may have even been able to turn a small profit before prices turned against you. The problem is that both of these situations would have left you on the sidelines just as prices were getting ready to make their way to all time highs.

You may have been savvy enough to keep watching and then enter again when prices broke free of their consolidation triangle at $1.25 in mid 2000. However, I find that being stopped out shortly after entering tends to change your psychology just enough to

give way to some fear, as well as, raise a little doubt that prices may
not be as strong as originally thought. After being stopped out with a
loss and then watching as prices fell by 40% over the next two years,
it's unlikely that most would then have had the discipline to re-enter at
the next opportunity. This slight hesitation is all it takes to leave you
on the sidelines as yet another stock sneaks away without you.

(Chart courtesy of Prophet.Net)

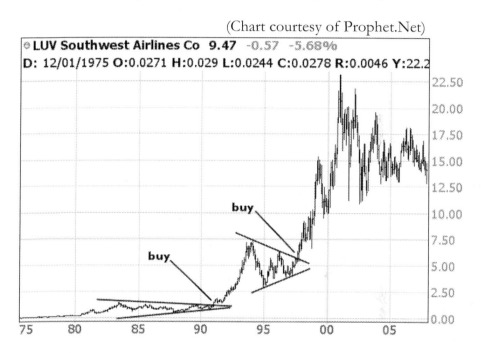

(Chart courtesy of Prophet.Net)

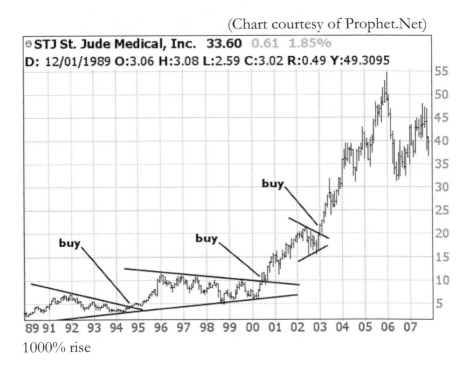

1000% rise

Clearly you can see how these consolidations play a major role in the markup phase. For Manipulator savvy investors you might look upon it as a catch 22 because consolidations will invariably delay the rise in prices for many years, however, the result of these delays is a much greater rise than would have otherwise happened without their presence.

Always remember the "WHY of prices". These consolidations are used by the Manipulators to shake the public out the market, to divert attention, and to discourage public buying. Why? So that they can maintain control and sneak prices higher right under your nose. Remember the diving board example. The higher they can get prices before the spring, the higher prices will ultimately go. So be patient and understand that markup is taking its time for a reason.

During markup it's only natural to want to be involved in your investment - making decisions, re-thinking your investment, second guessing yourself as you wait several years for prices to consolidate before rising again. But hold yourself back. Most often, the best action is to take is no action at all. The Manipulators are in charge. They are the ones who get to determine how long the accumulation base is, when the breakout occurs, how high prices will rise before a setback or consolidation, how long that consolidation will take and when the next breakout will occur. And then, how high the next rally will be and if there will be a second consolidation or not. Take solace in the fact that your new found ability to see into the future is enough. We know what will happen, we just don't know when. Sometimes your stock picks will rise 600% in 2 years and other times it will take 8 years for them to rise 200%.

You don't need to take a lot of action to make a lot of profits - you just need to put in the time. Now that's not to say that we turn our backs and forget about them for five years as some in the buy and hold camp would suggest. Or that we don't take action if the price chart offers up a signal to either add to our position or sell it altogether. But we do need to develop faith in the price cycle and the patience to allow the Manipulators to do what they need to do.

STOCK MARKET MYTH #6
Buy and Hold

Buy and hold is misleading term in that it leads one to a misguided sense of hope - a perception that stocks will continue to rise indefinitely over time. And, so long as you stay invested, then your portfolio will also go up indefinitely over time. The DOW 100 YEAR chart proves that as the market in general is much higher than it was in 1905 there are also extended periods during these last 100 years where the market appreciated very little.

Dates	Number of Years	Cumulative Return
1905 - 1921	16	4.51%
1929 - 1954	25	6.32%
1966 - 1983	17	1.62%
2000 - 2007	8 so far	0.00%

Please note that these are cumulative returns, not average annual returns. For example, had you been invested in the DOW 30 from 1966 – 1983, your return would have been (NOT 1.62% per year) but rather 1.62% total for the entire 17 year period. Which means that if your peak investing years (those years when you are contributing to most to your retirement portfolio) happen to coincide with one of these extended periods of flat returns, or coincide with the start of your retirement, I'm sure you'd come away truly disappointed. And, the so called "tried and true" strategy of buying and holding would have failed you miserably.

In fact, those who had invested "with the market" in 2000 would (as of 2007) have a 0.00% cumulative return for that entire 8 year period. How long does one have to wait for buy and hold to work, and how can you ever get back those 8 years of lost opportunity? Unfortunately – you can't.

Perhaps the single most important concept in the world of financial planning and portfolio management, but that which continues to be woefully neglected, is the ability and desire to sell. That's because when it comes to investment advice, SELL is a "four letter" word.

I suppose the main reason for this is the fact that all of the so-called experts, advisors and media personnel who make a living in this industry have drummed into our heads for decades that since no one can time the market, that our only and best opportunity is to stay invested. Of course, a second plausible explanation would be the fact that if financial planners, brokers, advisers and portfolio managers used this concept regularly (and especially during major market downturns), with large chunks of their customer's cash just sitting on the sidelines, they would significantly reduce their own commissions and trailer fees. Unfortunately, that scenario plays itself out anyway (with respect to commissions) as investors withdraw into their shells like frightened turtles, trying to avoid any extra exposure during 40% and 50% downturns. As well, fund portfolios that have been cut in half also produce half the trailer fees that they once did.

And, sure enough, just as soon as we are in the midst of a major meltdown, these are also the first people to say that because they aren't aware of anyone else who knew to sell out at the top, that they are therefore justified in their decision to stay invested for their customers. Their job then becomes one of reassuring those same customers that everything will work out in the long run. They just have to ride it out, and in time "it will come back – it always does". I don't know about you, but I don't want to watch my money lose 25% - 50% of its value and then have to just sit, watch and wait for countless years for it to recover. The stock market on whole has gone sideways for the last 8 years. And, if this current period of economic and stock market activity ends up being similar to the others described in Table 1, then we could be in store for possibly another 5 – 10 years of flat returns. Not a very attractive prospect, especially if you've been in the "market" these past 8 years and watched as your portfolio went down and up and then down again. Also, what if you're at that point in your career when you're ready to retire but your portfolio has been chopped by 30% - 50% and now isn't large enough to sustain you through your retirement years?

This is why the term "buy & hold" needs to be re-named buy, hold and sell. Because without the sell part, we're left to assume that all stocks rise and continue to rise indefinitely. And of course, we know that just isn't the case.

So, if you're not getting the results you desire, then it's time to make a change. And, the only way to get different results is to change those actions and habits that have led you to those less than ideal returns (Law of Cause & Effect).

Trend Lines

These are lines that investors draw on charts to give them an indication about which way prices are trending and, if in fact, prices have reversed direction from their previous trend. Many technical and even non-technical traders rely on trend lines to tell them when to buy and when to sell.

The Manipulators of course know this, and as such, take advantage of those who rely solely on this mechanical approach to investing. It is very easy for the Manipulators to control prices well enough to first allow a trend line to setup and then to allow for the violation of that same trend line. Not for the purposes of indicating a reversal of prices, but rather as a means to trick the public into selling on a temporary setback.

Manipulator savvy individuals, however, even though they do make the use of trend lines, recognize both of these situations and are able to incorporate all of their knowledge to more accurately determine if the break of a particular trend line is a real change in direction versus a manipulation of prices to shake free the public.

Many of the charts that we have looked at so far have revealed this trickery every time prices experienced significant, albeit "temporary", setbacks along their path to much higher prices. First, a trend is established by rising prices, and then a setback violates that trend indicating a possible change in direction. But then, prices rebound and continue on in their original upward direction. How do we know then if the break of trend is real or fabricated?

Although there are no exacts, no 100% when it comes to investing in equities, with knowledge of WHY prices move the way they do, you will be much better equipped to make accurate assessments. This will lead you to many more profitable decisions than those members of the investing public who strictly adhere to either technical or fundamental means alone.

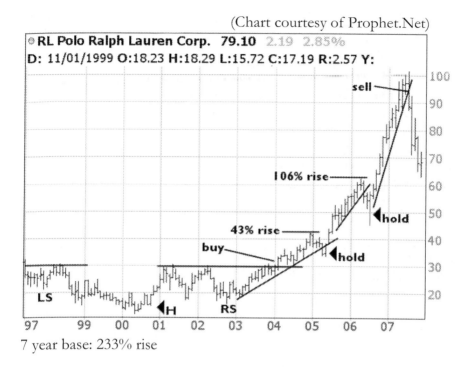

(Chart courtesy of Prophet.Net)

7 year base: 233% rise

For those investors who actually did buy low, the Manipulators of Ralph Lauren would have surely been successful at shaking the majority of them free during the break of the trend line at about $37.50 in 2005, as well as the other violation which came later at about $57 in 2006. And, I'm sure most would have been quite happy to get out with good profits at that time. Although, I'm just as sure, looking back now that they would be equally disappointed as prices eventually made their way above $100 in 2007.

How could they have known? They couldn't. They don't have a chance when the Manipulators are purposefully trying to deceive them.

How could you have known? Because you are aware of Manipulation. You are aware that a 7 year base in the bottom range is the recipe for a high rise not a mere rally. You are aware that the two setbacks that broke down and below their modestly sloping uptrend lines are signs of strength, not weakness. You are aware that encouraging, choppy, volatile price action is your signal to look for an opportunity to sell, none of which occurred prior to those two setbacks. And, you would have recognized that all of this price action (combined) prescribes for a much larger rise than that of just a mere 43% or 106%. Therefore, when prices did setback, you would have known that the setbacks had to be temporary and you would held on for higher prices. Your sell signal didn't come until prices broke through the steep uptrend line at approx. $93 in 2007. This is the kind of volatile price action that is indicative of distribution. Notice how prices rose from $60 up to $100 in the matter of just 8 months (during distribution) compared to the markup phase (2004 – mid 2006) where it took 2.5 years for prices to rise from $30 to $60.

(Chart courtesy of Prophet.Net)

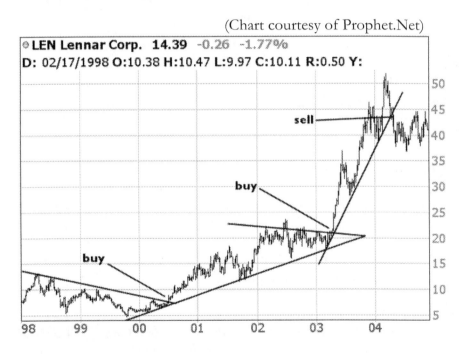

Keep in mind that the percentage rise we talk about as a means to determine how high prices may eventually travel is based on how strong the accumulation base appears, and is always referenced from the breakout of the base formation, not where you happened to enter the market. For example, had you entered Lennar Corp. in 2003 on the break of the triangle at about $22, the rally in prices from $22 to $52 in 2004 represented a rise of 136%. However, this is not the whole picture and certainly not how you should evaluate what the potential rise could be.

This point is very important because what might seem like a holding opportunity in one situation may, in fact, be a situation where you should be selling.

Let's look at another chart of Lennar to see if our perception changes.

(Chart courtesy of Prophet.Net)

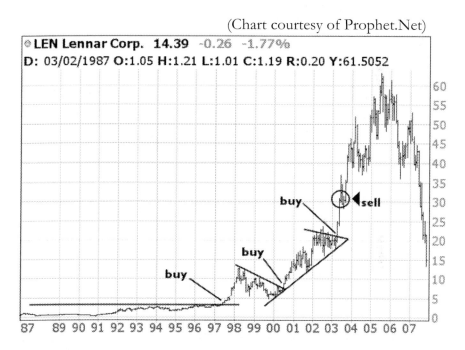

What appeared to be a good looking base on the 10 year chart of Lennar is in fact an incredibly strong base of 25 years (not all shown). And, what we thought was the base on the 10 year chart in fact turns out to be a consolidation triangle during markup. As in all cases, the longest term chart always provides the most accurate picture.

With this new perspective, you would have noticed the extremely steep run up in prices from $22 to $37 in 2003. And, knowing at that level, that prices had already risen 1133% off their base ($3.00 to $37), you would have certainly been looking for a chance to sell at your first opportunity (which came when prices setback in mid 2003).

This is another reminder of just how important it is to view all of the available price history. If a picture tells a thousand words, why would you settle for just half a picture? The more price information that you can incorporate into your decision making process, the more accurate will be your decisions and the more successful your investments. Even though we don't know how high a markup will take us, we do know that a multi-year accumulation base, along with consolidations and setbacks during early markup will almost always produce a rise in prices of at least 200%. This is the case for all stocks.

(Chart courtesy of Prophet.Net)

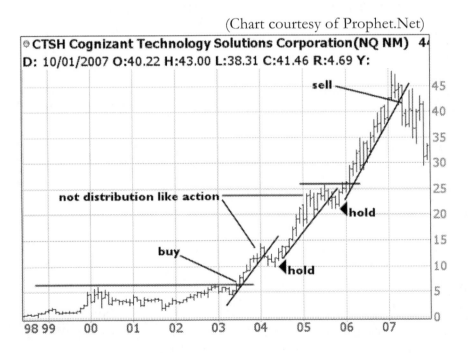

The chart of Cognizant Technology really shows us the power of trend lines when used in conjunction with price cycle philosophy. The breakout of the base gave us our first entry opportunity to enter at approx. $7.00 in 2003. The setback after prices made their way up to $14 later that year would have had most investors and certainly most technical traders running for the exits on the break of the uptrend line.

However, every price cycle savvy investor realizes that a 5.5 year base will (in almost every case) support a rise much greater than a mere 100%. As well, viewing the chart from a price cycle perspective would have also revealed that the price action that preceded the setback was not distribution-like action, therefore, any setback had to be temporary in nature. In this case we would have been holding, (even though the trend line was violated), expecting a much greater rise. Prices did proceed higher, ultimately setting up a modestly sloping trend line throughout 2004 and 2005 which is exactly what we would have expected during the early stages of markup. And, as luck would have it (yes, sometimes we do need some luck), prices continued higher without any major setbacks. As prices moved higher, we continued to adjust our trend lines which ended up becoming steeper as prices made their way hundreds of percent above their base. After prices reached $47.50, they finally started to trend lower. At that point, the steep upward move combined with a 578% rise off the base would have triggered our senses to be on the lookout for a selling opportunity.

A stop-sell placed in advance and moved week by week, higher and higher, following the steep trend line up, would have given us our protection in case of any sudden drop in prices. Prices finally broke through to the downside in 2007 at about $42.50. That would have provided a 507% profit in about 4 years. Had we not been aware that prices move the way they do for a reason, we would surely have joined the masses sitting on the sidelines and watching as yet another stock rose to all time highs without us. Or perhaps, if we were technical in nature, and we were smart enough to have bought on the breakout of the base, then we would surely have sold out just as quickly at $12.50 on the break of the trend line (with a 78% profit). Pretty good, but it's no 507%.

Now that we were out of this market, we would be staying away and looking for opportunities elsewhere. Prices had now risen a long way off the bottom and no matter how strong the base is, it becomes way too risky to even think about entering up at these levels. Time to go bottom fishing again.

Trend lines can be powerful tools and they should not be overlooked, however, they should also **NOT** be used as a stand-alone indicator either. What gives them their power is YOU. Your ability to read and decipher long term charts, to understand the WHY of prices, and to determine when the breaking of a trend line is real and when it is manipulated fantasy.

(Chart courtesy of Prophet.Net)

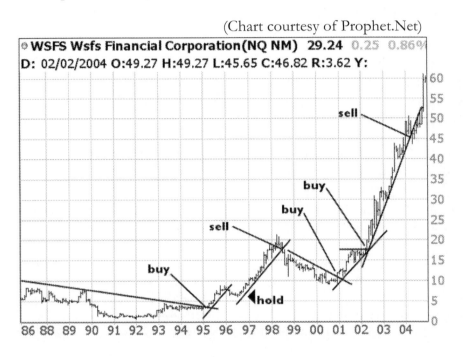

Lots of study and practice over time will give you the ability to predict the future and take back control of your invested dollars. But remember, as much as we make predictions and assessments about what we think will happen, we always defer to the price action recorded on the long term chart to give us our cues to take action. The price action is a direct representation of everything that is going on in any particular stock and, therefore, always provides us with the best insight for making decisions. There is a fine line between knowing that prices will go up and knowing **WHEN** they will go up. Don't get ahead of yourself. The one thing we will never know about prices is **WHEN**, therefore, let the chart dictate the when of price movement. Your job is to be ready to act when it gives you the signal.

(Chart courtesy of Prophet.Net)

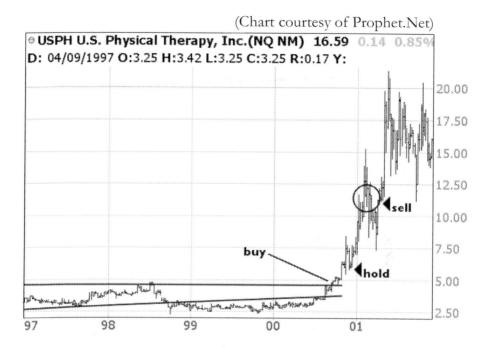

USPH U.S. Physical Therapy, Inc.(NQ NM) 16.59 0.14 0.85%
D: 04/09/1997 O:3.25 H:3.42 L:3.25 C:3.25 R:0.17 Y:

As the markup phase for US Physical Therapy proceeded, prices became extremely active almost immediately after breaking out of their base in 2000. You would have probably been able to hold through the first setback from $8.50 down to $6.00 knowing that this large of a base (9 years – not all shown) would most surely produce a larger rise. However, when prices raced their way up to $15 in a matter of months, (even though this only represented a 200% rise off its base) this extremely violent price activity should have had you looking to sell at your next opportunity. The break of this steep trend in prices in early 2001 would have been your signal.

Violent price action with big daily volumes and large price swings is your sign to get out. This is the kind of action that gets the public interested. When enough of the outstanding shares trade hands from strong (Manipulators) to weak (public), prices will become extremely unstable and have nowhere to go but down. In this case, prices did eventually go higher, but it's just too risky to try and hold through these violent price moves.

Just as we must be patient and wait for our opportunities to present themselves, we must also take what the Manipulators are willing to offer and move on. Again, investing will always be an inexact science. Sometimes prices will rise 200% but start to appear choppy so you'll sell when the trend line breaks only then to see them quickly turn around and race to all time highs 1000% off their base. And, other times prices will appear as though they are advancing slowly and setting up a modestly sloping trend line, so you'll hold through the break of the trend line only to watch as prices continue to fall all the way back down to their base. The best we can do is to take in all of the information we can from the long term chart, buy on breakouts of accumulation bases and consolidation periods during early markup and then wait and watch as prices proceed higher. It will always be harder to sell than to buy, but by using your new found price cycle perspective, at least you'll be able to sway the odds in your favour.

Sometimes prices will go higher than we think, other times not. Sometimes markup will last 6 months, and sometimes 6 years, but it is not for us to judge. The long term price chart will reveal all we need to know.

(Chart courtesy of Prophet.Net)

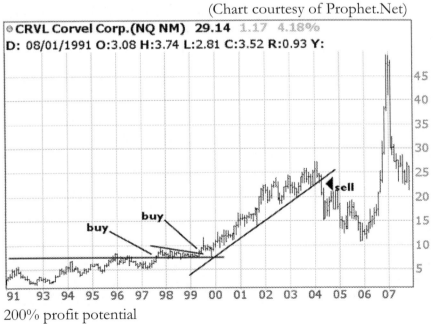

200% profit potential

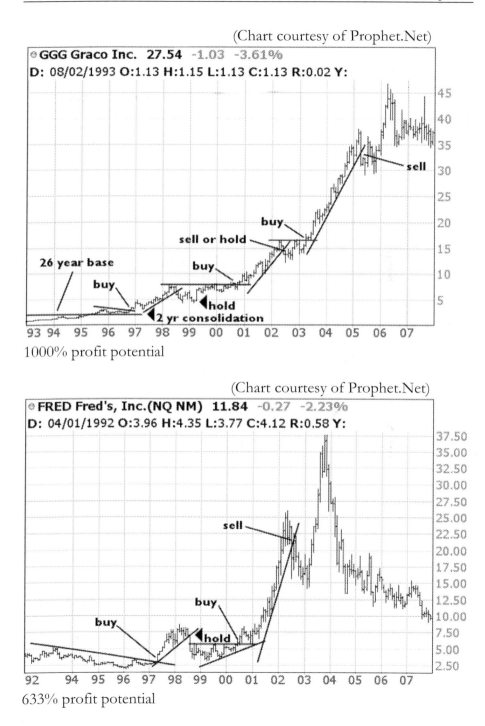

(Chart courtesy of Prophet.Net)

GGG Graco Inc. 27.54 -1.03 -3.61%
D: 08/02/1993 O:1.13 H:1.15 L:1.13 C:1.13 R:0.02 Y:

26 year base

buy

buy

sell or hold

buy

sell

hold

2 yr consolidation

45
40
35
30
25
20
15
10
5

93 94 95 96 97 98 99 00 01 02 03 04 05 06 07

1000% profit potential

(Chart courtesy of Prophet.Net)

FRED Fred's, Inc.(NQ NM) 11.84 -0.27 -2.23%
D: 04/01/1992 O:3.96 H:4.35 L:3.77 C:4.12 R:0.58 Y:

sell

buy

buy

hold

37.50
35.00
32.50
30.00
27.50
25.00
22.50
20.00
17.50
15.00
12.50
10.00
7.50
5.00
2.50

92 94 95 96 97 98 99 00 01 02 03 04 05 06 07

633% profit potential

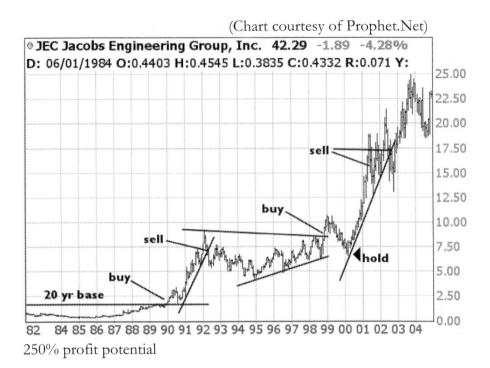

(Chart courtesy of Prophet.Net)

250% profit potential

Setbacks

A setback is defined as a temporary reversal in price, the key word being <u>temporary</u>. Most investors fear setbacks because they signal weakness and lead to an uncertainty about selling as they try to guess whether or not prices will recover and go higher.

They have this uncertainty because they are not aware of the big picture, the man-made price cycle. They do not know the difference between markup and distribution. They are not aware of why prices move the way they do. They are not aware that prices require rest periods along the way in order to sustain higher prices in the future. They are not aware that setbacks are good for the purposes of shaking out the public, which results in the Manipulators being able to extend their control over prices, ultimately driving them much higher.

Setbacks should be welcomed as they provide us with signals and clues as to what the Manipulators have been up to so far, and what they are planning to do in the future. Setbacks used in combination with formations are extremely revealing. Early on in markup they help us to confirm possible entry points, and later in markup they give us evidence that large rallies may be close at hand.

Often times the biggest rallies will follow the biggest setbacks and just as often these large setbacks will occur half way along into the markup phase. Just when you think that prices have gone as high as they can, a severe mid-level setback occurs, confirming your belief. But what you thought was the top, turns out to be just a temporary setback in advance of a dramatic rally to even higher highs and distribution (refer to the Source Capital chart below).

Remember, the Manipulators are trying to shake you free from their coat-tails during markup, so it only makes sense that at that point when they are ready to move prices a lot higher and, at a faster rate, they would want to get rid of as many investors as possible. Fewer investors means more control on the way up and the higher they will ultimately be able to push prices. Also, with all those investors on the sidelines, it ensures a ready supply of buyers when it comes time for them to unload in the top range.

(Chart courtesy of Prophet.Net)

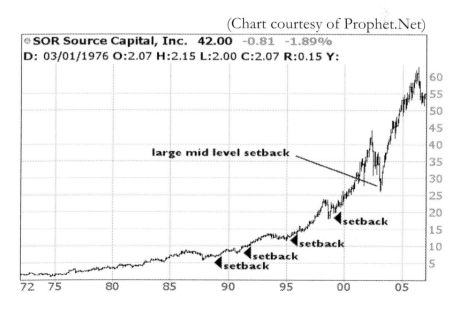

Please note that I'm not suggesting that you try and hold through a large mid-level setback as seen here with Source (previous page), especially after prices have risen hundreds of percent off their base. It is important though to be fully aware of all the Manipulator's techniques and tricks to ensure that you are prepared and ready to act when such a scenario presents itself.

(Chart courtesy of Prophet.Net)

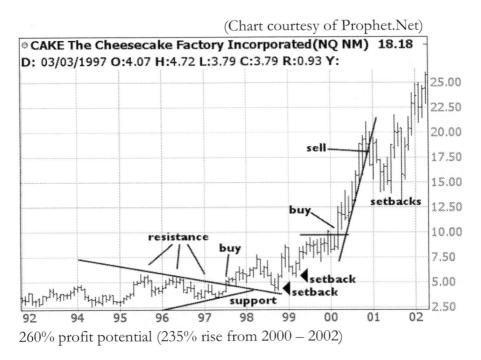

260% profit potential (235% rise from 2000 – 2002)

Don't fall in love with stocks. Don't fall in love with industries. Don't fall in love with sectors. The only thing that you should concern yourself with (other than its long term chart) is with the soundness of the company. Once you're satisfied that the company is sound (financially stable), the long term chart will provide you with all the information you need.

Where was your money invested in 2000, in microchips or cheesecake? In retrospect, The Cheesecake Factory would have been the way to go. The 5 year accumulation base was your signal that a significant amount of internal pressure had been built-up and the resulting strength had to be released in the form of rising prices.

After breakout in mid 1997, prices made their way to new highs only to experience several setbacks. Setbacks following breakouts of multi-year accumulation bases are almost always a sure sign that markup is underway, especially when prices bounce off a line of resistance turned support (as shown here in late 1998).

Prices continued higher despite setbacks and consolidations along the way, just as you'd expect. However, now having reached $21 in late 2000, (which represented a 300% rise off their base), the Manipulators once again realized they had better slow things down for a while if they ever hoped to reach even higher prices in the future. The severe double setback that ensued in 2001, first down to $13.50, and then back down to $13, must have been frightening enough for most of the public to bail out. This is evidenced by the fact that prices quickly recovered all of their lost ground on their way back up to even higher highs in 2002.

In this case, the wise course of action would have been to sell when the steep uptrend line was broken at about $18 in 2000, even though you may have felt that prices would probably go higher based on the size of the base and the setbacks and consolidations that added even more strength during early markup. A sell order placed at approx. $18 would have netted you a 260% return in 3 years had you caught the original breakout at $5.00.

Whenever an uptrend line changes from being moderately sloped (30 to 45 degrees), to one that approaches the vertical as seen here in 2000, it's time to look for an opportunity to sell. The steeper the trend line, the more attention it should draw as you move to protect your profits by raising your stop-sell order frequently as prices rise with the trend.

Also, Cheesecake Factory is the perfect example of what we talked about earlier with respect to how much profit you can and should expect to earn when investing in stocks. Keep in mind that this substantial 260% profit represents less than half of the overall run-up. The total rise from breakout to summit was 686% (from $5.00 to $39.28 when it peaked in 2006 - not shown).

138

(Chart courtesy of Prophet.Net)

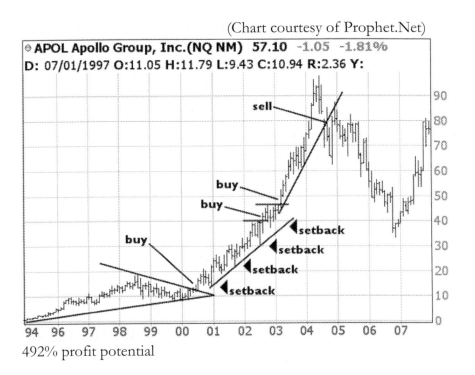

492% profit potential

Apollo Group is the consummate example of setbacks used in series to discourage and dissuade. Earlier we likened the building-up of internal pressure of a long consolidation, similar to that of blowing many continuous breaths into a balloon until it swelled, and then releasing all of that pressure at once to produce a large rise in prices. Well, setbacks in series operate in a different manner.

In both cases, the goal of the Manipulators is higher prices over time. Using many setbacks, one after another, would be like releasing just enough of the built-up pressure to slowly propel prices a little higher. With less pressure though, prices would slowly drift backwards in the form of a setback until the next few breaths pump it back up to gain some support and to keep it from falling further. Then the next release would send prices slightly higher than the last rally. And on and on... Each time prices setback they gain a little more strength, each time prices rally they lose a little bit of their strength. The net result is a conservation of the internal strength to enable prices to continue higher on their way to distribution. The combination of build-up and release, setback and rally, many times, over and over, ultimately achieves the same goal as that of a long consolidation channel or triangle.

The benefit to you as an investor is that without any <u>severe setbacks</u> along the way to cause you to sell, you are able to hang on longer thus enabling you to ride the markup phase higher, resulting in larger profits.

(Chart courtesy of Prophet.Net)

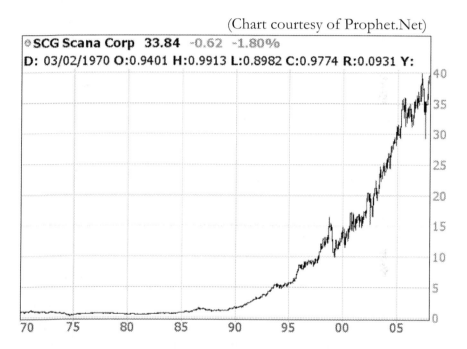

With respect to Scana Corp., how many public investors do you think could have held on during this roller coaster ride to the top? Probably not very many, and certainly none who weren't aware of the man-made price cycle. Now let's take a closer look.

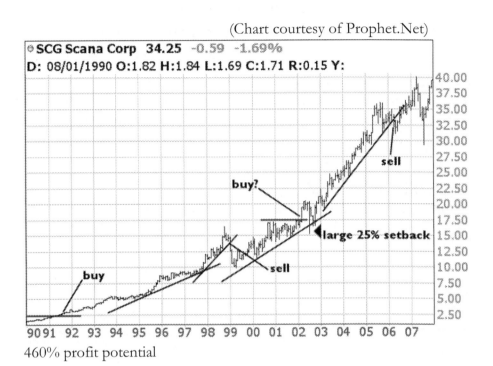

(Chart courtesy of Prophet.Net)

460% profit potential

One thing is for sure though, this 21 year base (see previous page) for Scana Corp. warrants more than just a mere rally. The move in price from $2.50 - $17.00 over the course of 7.5 years would have probably had you looking for a sell signal, even though you might have expected a base of this size to support a larger move than just 600%. Had you sold in early 1999 on the break of the steep uptrend line, then you may have been watching for another opportunity to get back in. After selling and following the subsequent price action you would have quickly realized that the price action that preceded the setback in 1999 was probably not encouraging enough or lasted for a long enough period of time to enable the Manipulators to sell the millions of shares that they had acquired during the 21 year base. However, it is always wise to walk away with a significant profit and look for your next accumulation breakout, than to try to enter and exit during the more volatile action of upper markup.

(Chart courtesy of Prophet.Net)

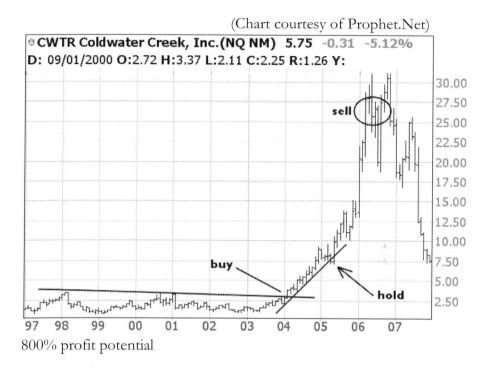

CWTR Coldwater Creek, Inc.(NQ NM) 5.75 -0.31 -5.12%
D: 09/01/2000 O:2.72 H:3.37 L:2.11 C:2.25 R:1.26 Y:

800% profit potential

Sometimes there is so much internal pressure built-up that the Manipulators don't require the use of multiple setbacks or major consolidations along the way. Sometimes there is so much pressure, that when finally released, prices explode straight up, never looking back, never pausing until they reach their top. This is the case with Coldwater Creek and its 7 year base (and this is a good example of how there are no absolutes when it comes to investing).

But, with that said, do you see how and why they did use one setback early on in the markup phase to near perfection? After reaching new highs at approx. $9.00 in 2005, the Manipulators withdrew their support and allowed prices to fall below the uptrend line that had established itself throughout 2004. This price action would have been enough to shake free anyone who had entered the market earlier on a technical buy.

Technical trading would have failed them though because (without price cycle awareness), they were left only to rely on their technical indicators, which would have told them to sell when the uptrend line was violated. I'm sure they would have been extremely happy with a 100% - 200% profit depending on where they got in. However, I don't think they would have looked upon it as much of a success, had they seen the rise that they missed out on. Had you entered on the breakout of the base at approx. $3.00, you would have been given no signal to get out until prices had reached approx. $27. A multi-year accumulation base will almost always produce a much larger rise than a mere 100% - 200%. In this case it turned out to be a 900% rise off the base.

This is why it is imperative that you understand and employ price cycle philosophy rather than just technical indicators when it comes to making your investment decisions. Technical indicators are right half the time, which means that they are also wrong half the time. Coldwater Creek is not an opportunity that you want included in the wrong half.

So far we have dealt with the "WHAT". What the Manipulators are doing in order to achieve their fantastic results. We have talked about their motivation, GREED. We have talked about the man-made price cycle and how each of the four phases plays a crucial role to the whole process. Now we'll talk about how the entire process would fall apart if not for the public's insatiable desire to buy high and sell low.

- How the Manipulators are able to get you out of the market at the bottom when prices are low and get you back in at the top when prices are topping out.

- How they are able to time and time again buy at the bottom and sell at the top for incredible profits.

- How they are able to produce these incredible results over and over with reliable precision.

- How they are able to manipulate you and the rest of the public into believing that if you just keep trying you will get eventually get it right.

It's hard enough to pick a winner, get in at the right price, wait out the ups and downs, and then eventually sell for a profit before it falls back. Now add to that the fact that there are people involved in Manipulating the price of every stock you invest in, trying to trick you into making wrong decisions, and you can see how the cards are stacked against you. And, why you have little chance of success unless you get on board.

If the markup phase is similar to our search for buried treasure with all of the inevitable obstacles, delays and pitfalls along our path, then finding the location where "X" marks the spot, is where we finally get to reap our rewards. This is our treasure chest – this is **distribution.**

Distribution

How do they do it? How do the Manipulators manage to get the public excited and buying high, after prices have in many cases risen over 300%, 500% or even 1000% off the bottom. And, in spite of the fact that every investor claims to know and practice the universal law of investing – "buy low and sell high".

During distribution, the Manipulators #1 weapon is encouraging price action. But what really makes this all possible is the one trait that is shared by most every investor - GREED. They want to make money and they want to make it fast.

The only way they can do this is to trade stocks that are experiencing extreme volatility and volumes. And, the only stocks that show this type of movement are stocks that are in distribution. What a coincidence – NOT!

Why is that? Why are these the only stocks exhibiting this type of volatility? Because the Manipulators are the ones who are controlling prices. They know what the public wants. They know what causes the public to sell (at the bottom) and what causes them to buy up at the top. So why not give them (you) exactly what they want. In turn they are only too happy to fill those buy orders with sell orders of their own. Not coincidentally, the huge volumes, large daily price swings, and high prices are also the type of price action that the media thrives on. The higher prices go, and the faster they go, the more attention they are paid. And, since most of the public get their investing inspiration from TV, newsletters, web sites, analysts and/or from the newspaper, there is never of lack of buying interest in the top range. It's like sharks during a feeding frenzy - the more meat that gets thrown into the water, the greater the number of sharks that show up, and the more frenzied the feeding.

I can't tell you how many times I have woken up in the morning to the "experts" on TV, only to check the long term price history of their buy recommendations to find that the very stocks they were recommending (because of good earnings or some other fundamental tidbit) had already risen over 500%, 600% or even 800% off their bases. These stocks were invariably trading at or near their all time highs yet these "experts" were recommending that you buy them. Is there any doubt that the Manipulators will have trouble finding investors to sell to in the top range?

The Manipulators fire-up the public into buying into a big rally. The public buys driving prices higher and higher as the media catches wind and reports on it. More and more public investors become aware and they too jump on the bandwagon trying to get a piece of the action – fast, easy money. All the while the Manipulators are selling. After some time and a lot of volatile price action in the top range, the Manipulators are sold out and the public is left holding the bag at the top. And, it's a heavy bag to hold up. Let's take a closer look at how they accomplish this feat.

Quite simply, distribution is the opposite of accumulation. This is when the Manipulators are selling (unfortunately to the unsuspecting public). Remember the analogy we drew earlier about the base runner stealing second base, and how we likened the markup phase to that of the base runner sneaking his way towards second without anyone noticing. Well, taking this example one step further, distribution then could be likened to the base runner now sprinting towards second. This is when prices are moving quickly, there is a lot of attention and excitement being paid to a stock. There are big daily swings, with prices hitting new highs, falling back and then rallying again to even higher highs. There are huge daily volumes, and the stock is being reported on daily in the newspaper and on TV. This is the excitement and fast money making opportunity that so many investors are looking for. This is the Manipulators biggest TRAP - this is what gets you to buy high and allows them to unload at the top.

To paraphrase Andrew Tobias, "Think of a circus performer on a tightrope. The higher the wire, the more we take notice and the louder we applaud. Bring it back down to just a few feet off the ground, and people lose interest – but it's obviously safer. Why don't we see that with stocks?"

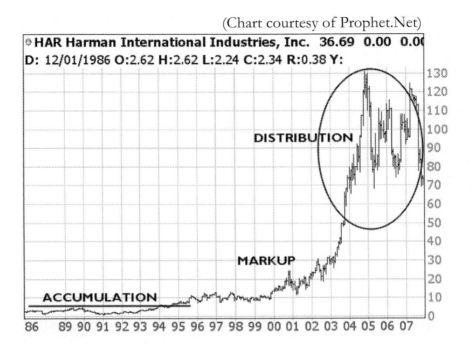

(Chart courtesy of Prophet.Net)

HAR Harman International Industries, Inc. 36.69 0.00 0.0(
D: 12/01/1986 O:2.62 H:2.62 L:2.24 C:2.34 R:0.38 Y:

DISTRIBUTION

MARKUP

ACCUMULATION

86   89 90 91 92 93 94 95 96 97 98 99 00 01 02 03 04 05 06 07

130
120
110
100
90
80
70
60
50
40
30
20
10
0

With Harman, look at the waves of encouraging, choppy price action in the top range. Prices rally quickly to new highs only to fall back, but then quickly rally right back up again. This continued choppy up and down price action is the perfect example of distribution. This is the kind of action that draws the attention of the analysts and media. This is what gets the public excited. This is why the Manipulators will always have any easy time selling out at the top after having bought in at extremely low levels.

Look at the difference in price action between the different phases of the price cycle. Accumulation is extremely quiet and discouraging over many years causing you to overlook a bargain. The slow steady action of markup, drawn out over many years is again not exciting enough to grab your attention and, if it does, you are eventually worn down by all of the setbacks and consolidations along the way causing you to lose faith and sell. But then, prices start to get really exciting, volumes are way up, and the media is talking about the stock regularly and attributing some piece of news or fundamental statistic to give reason why prices should be so encouraging. Then the analysts come out in droves to affirm their buy recommendations, and raise their price targets for this stock even though prices have already risen over 900% off the bottom.

Can you see what is happening? Can you see why you don't stand a chance? The only time that prices are encouraging and active, and making bigger gains in a shorter period of time is in the top range. And since most of the public only feels good about a stock when it is acting in this manner, you can see why the Manipulators will always have someone to sell to at the top. The public is trying to get their hands on as many shares as they can, and the Manipulators are cashing out for huge profits.

During situations where you were about to buy some shares in a stock, have you ever stopped to ask yourself who is selling these shares to me and why? Obviously they think prices are going down – why? Because they have a different perspective - because they have manipulated your emotions and better judgment causing you to make wrong decisions - because they have control over prices.

Watsco Inc. (next page) provides an excellent illustration of price action and how it varies from accumulation through markup and on into distribution. At the bottom, prices are extremely quiet with low volumes, which tend to travel in a mostly sideways manner for many years (discouraging). In contrast, markup sees increased activity as prices slowly rise over time with a slight increase in volumes (slightly encouraging/slightly discouraging). Distribution on the other hand is indicative of quickly rising prices and huge daily volumes (completely encouraging).

(Chart courtesy of Prophet.Net)

Had you entered this market after the breakout from the base back in 1992 and/or again during markup you would certainly have sold out long before prices ever reached their peak.

Be aware that all charts will present a different picture, however, the essence of what is happening and WHY, is always the same. Fast rising, volatile, price action hundreds of percent above the base is your signal to sell because that's what the Manipulators are doing - selling.

Distribution has two purposes that are easily recognized on any price chart. The Manipulators need to make the price activity appear promising to get investors interested and buying. Otherwise they would have no one to sell to. Their two goals of this phase are intertwined, and could be actually looked upon as one goal – to sell high after having bought really low. I have broken it down into two separate points though to show you where you fit in.

1. To get you excited and buying in the top range,
2. so they can sell out to YOU and realize their profits.

They cannot do one without the other. If you come to believe and trust that the Manipulators control the markets and are the ones who are making the majority of the profits, then you can see how this process HAS to take place. It is the very nature of how the markets operate. Every stock has a fixed number of outstanding shares owned by various individuals, companies, mutual funds, brokerages, pension funds, etc. In order for someone to sell their stock, someone else has to be on the other end of the transaction buying it.

What this means is that these two parties are at exact opposite ends of the spectrum in their estimate of where the stock will go next. One believes that prices will fall so they are selling and the other feels that prices will rise so they are buying and, since prices can only go one way – one of these participants is about to be very disappointed.

If you owned a lot of stock in the bottom range, (by that I mean millions of shares), how on earth would you be able to sell it if prices appeared weak and discouraging as they did for Celgene Corp. (next page) from 1987 - 1999? No one would want to buy it from you because everyone would be of the same opinion, that the stock was weak and therefore likely wouldn't go any higher. Besides, it wouldn't make sense from a profit perspective either.

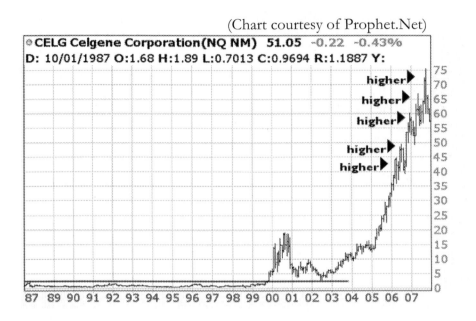

CELG Celgene Corporation(NQ NM) 51.05 -0.22 -0.43%
D: 10/01/1987 O:1.68 H:1.89 L:0.7013 C:0.9694 R:1.1887 Y:

But, what if you were able to keep the price action showing promise, by means of big daily price swings, big daily volumes, and consistently higher highs (2006 – 2007)? In this situation, it would probably be quite easy to unload your millions of shares, wouldn't it? Well, this is exactly what the Manipulators do. They give the public exactly what they are looking for and, in turn, are only too happy to fill their buy orders. Sure, some investors may get lucky and turn a profit by getting in and out at the right time in the top range, but the vast majority will end up buying high, HOLDING, and then selling much lower, later, when the majority of shares have changed to weak hands – hands that are unable to support prices.

Is it just by chance that the very action that most people find appealing, the wild, violent, choppy price action with big daily volumes and higher highs is always in the top range, and the quiet, boring sideways action, the type of action most people ignore (the type of action you find during the accumulation phase) is always in the bottom range.

Your emotions are causing you to do the exact opposite of what so many people say they do, but never really actually do, which is to buy low and sell high.   Referring to Denison Mining, buying low doesn't mean buying at $9.00 on the large setback in 2007 and then trying to sell at $13 a couple of months later. It means buying at $1.00 on the breakout of the base, and selling at $6.00, two years later. It means being patient along with the Manipulators and allowing them to do what they need to do. In the case of Denison, it means waiting two years for a 500% rise.

(Chart courtesy of Prophet.Net)

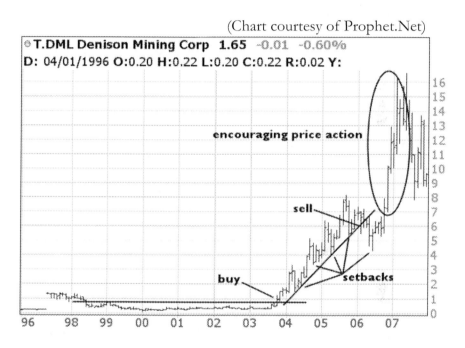

T.DML Denison Mining Corp 1.65 -0.01 -0.60%
D: 04/01/1996 O:0.20 H:0.22 L:0.20 C:0.22 R:0.02 Y:

        Look at the encouraging price action in the top range for Denison. This is the kind of action that gets the attention of both the media and the investing public. The trouble is that the Manipulators are all too aware of that same fact. How often does the media report on a company and sing their praises when their prices are flat lining as they were for Denison from 1996 – 2003? They don't, and that lack of attention and praise is exactly the kind of discouraging action that the Manipulators count on to keep the public on the sidelines. The net result for them is to accumulate a large position over time during the accumulation phase and then patiently wait for markup and distribution to unload and reap their veritable windfall.

You might say that there is no way anyone would wait that long for profits. Why not, millions of people have invested billions of dollars in mutual funds, bond funds, RRSP's, and 401K plans for their retirement with no intention of touching their investment for 10 or 20 years or more with the hopes of averaging 7 - 10% a year over the long run (buy & hold myth). Is 5 – 10 years too long for the Manipulators to wait for a 500% - 2500% return on their investment? I think not. What are the main reasons the public continues to buy at the top?

1. The public (for the most part) don't bother to consult price charts, especially long term charts. Without taking this simple first step to evaluate any stock, how can they possibly know if a stock is trading at a price that is high, low or somewhere in between? How can they possibly know if they are getting a bargain or paying top dollar? Why is it that the media, when they do refer to price charts only ever show you one day or one week or one year of price history? The only way to know if any particular stock is a bargain is to check the long term price chart (10 - 20 years worth of price history, if available).

2. The public tends to get caught up in media hype and count on analysts and so-called market experts to tell them what is hot and what is not. Unfortunately, this information has very little to do with finding a stock in the lower price range because quiet discouraging price action is not exciting and, therefore, not news worthy. Did you know that during March 2000 when the DOW and NASDAQ where nearing all time highs, the collective buy recommendations by some of Wall Street's top analysts were at 74%, whereas those same analysts were offering less than 1% sell recommendations on the stocks they were covering. And we all know what happened next.

3. The public tends to have a short time perspective – much too short. They are impatient and greedy and are always looking for ways to make a quick buck. And, this time perspective has become even more skewed to the short end of the scale due to the unbelievably quick markup so many popular stocks enjoyed during 1999. The day trading phenomenon cast a new

expectation about time and money, which continues to fuel this impatience and make an even easier time of it for the Manipulators to coax you in at the top. In 1960, the average holding period for stocks was 8 years. In 2002, the average holding time was 11 months.

STOCK MARKET MYTH #7
<u>A Stock Moves Based on its Fundamental Valuation</u>

Or, in other words, the price of a stock moves up and down based on fair market value as dictated by its earnings, product line, competitive factors, book value, balance sheet, debt levels, pending lawsuits, effects of government intervention, analysts forecasts, consumer spending, global demand, interest rates, value of the dollar, cost of raw materials, inventory levels, etc, etc, etc...

First of all, even if this were true, unless you have an advanced economics degree, how could you possibly ever expect to be able to research and gather all of the information, news, and financial statistics that are current and relevant to any particular stock. Combine and give each bit of info its due weighting of importance and then interpret all the available data which is being updated on a daily basis to come up with an actionable decision whether to buy, hold, sell or stay away. That would be a daunting task. In fact, even the expert money managers who make a career of it by managing hundreds of millions of dollars (of other people's money in mutual funds) prove every year that they can't do it. Why is it that fundamentals are the preferred approach to stock market investing when over 80% of these money managers are not even able to beat the market, year in and year out? So if they can't do it with all of their economics degrees and decades of experience, what makes you think you can?

Fortunately for us, we don't need a degree to succeed – just a desire to learn and an awareness of the man-made price cycle. Stock prices move according to what the Manipulators require – period. If prices are acting volatile and trading in the upper price range, then it's because the Manipulators have a large holding that they need to sell off, and they know that if price action is encouraging, then the public will buy no matter what the price. It's as simple as that.

Fundamental analysis is characterized by people who gather, decipher and interpret mounds of data in an effort to make profitable investment decisions. This seems like a very rational and logical way to go about determining a company's value and growth potential and hence what its stock price will likely do in the future. But, we know that the public's emotional bias does not act in sync with these facts. If somehow we were all able to remove emotion from our lives and make decisions based purely on logic (like Mr. Spock) then the markets would be a reflection of that and also act in a very logical and rational manner (as some economists would have you believe).

But the fact that emotion can never be taken out of the human equation guarantees that stocks and markets in general will always act in an irrational manner. Therefore, making investment decisions using strictly numbers, data and logic will leave you with less than the total picture and will not allow you to stack the odds in your favour.

Remember:

"The market can remain illogical, longer than you can remain solvent."

John Maynard Keynes

If the markets did act rationally and moved based on fundamentals, then wouldn't those same fundamentals offer a signal to these very same money managers of impending 40 – 50% drops in both individual stocks and markets in general? But for some reason these fundamentalists never seem to be able to spot a major market crash in the making and sell out of their holdings.

If the data that they rely on isn't even relevant and accurate enough to uncover major stock market moves in advance, then how could they possibly use that same data to determine if stocks and markets are going to rise or fall by 5 – 10%? Every stock market crash and subsequent public portfolio meltdown is constant and recurring proof that fundamental analysis is not the best method with which to make investment decisions.

And, if you need more convincing of why prices move (for reasons other than fundamental) then just look to recent history. Look at any of the hundreds and hundreds of stocks that rose to unsustainable highs in 1999 and 2000 during the tech bubble.

One example that most investors are aware of is when Nortel stock went racing up to all time highs in March 2000. Did the fundamental statistics for that company indicate that $120/share was a fair and accurate price for that stock, at the time? Did its earnings and other data suggest that $120 was fair market value? Of course not. No expert of the day would have told you so. In fact, based on the fundamentals at that time, most experts were saying that Nortel's price should have been closer to $60/share or less to indicate fair market value. But that didn't keep it from reaching $120/share did it? Why? Because a stock's price doesn't move based on what the fundamentals say, it moves based on what the public gets excited about.

Combining this fundamental approach to investing, with a buy and hold mentality, results in a recipe for disaster. Unfortunately, this disaster shows itself by way of the recurring deterioration of the public's retirement portfolio.

A word about **DIVIDENDS**. Most fundamentalists will recommend you buy dividend paying stocks. I'm here to say that you should never buy a stock because it pays a dividend. Buy a stock because it has a base that will support a high rise. Buy a stock that is breaking out of a long accumulation base or consolidation period during early markup. And, if that same stock happens to pay a dividend too, then consider it a bonus. But, never use the fact that a stock pays a dividend as criteria for buying it in the first place. Dividends are a bonus not a reason.

(Chart courtesy of Prophet.Net)

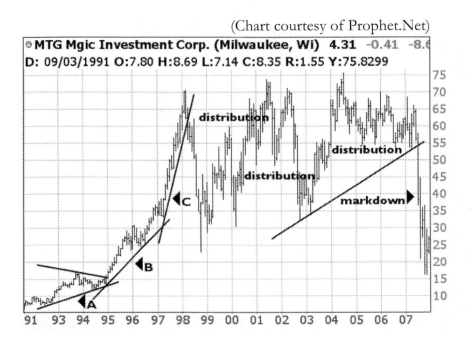

MGIC Investment Corp. is a good example of a multi-year distribution top. Your sell signal came in 1998 at about $60 when the steepest trend line was broken after having been adjusted steeper and steeper (A to B to C). That last, most violent steep rise (C), in combination with an overall 366% rise off the base ($15 to $70) was your clue to get out even though distribution had just begun.

Although prices did eventually go higher, they only made their way up to $73 and that took 3.5 more years of volatile price action with a 67% price drop in the interim. Had you gotten greedy and been hanging on for a higher high, you would have had to ride out some serious swings to the down side which would have most likely resulted in your selling out at a much lower price.

As evidenced by the large distribution top (1997 – 2007), the Manipulators were eventually able to sell out of their holdings but not without a lot of effort (10 years worth). Emotions are the rule of the day and as long as we humans have them, so too will they be taken advantage of by people who have the resources and the ability to do it.

> **The rule for you is**; buy when the Manipulators are finished buying and sell when they are starting to sell. Or, in other words, buy at the end of accumulation and sell at the beginning of distribution or distribution-like action.

There are many things that a long term chart can tell us about was has happened in the past, as well as, what is about to happen in the future. However, as mentioned earlier, there are a few things that we will only ever learn after they have taken place.

1. When the breakout will occur,
2. how high prices will go,
3. and how long it will take for them to get there.

These are all questions that are only answered with moving prices. In the case of Deckers Outdoor Corp. (next page), a stop-buy placed in advance would have been filled on the breakout of the base at $5.00 in 2003. Just as a stop-buy was the correct way to enter this market, a sell on the break of the uptrend line at approx. $38 after prices had risen 880% ($5 - $49), was the correct way to exit it.

This is a great example of how you can make incredible profits even though you're invested for only a small portion of the overall rise. Prices for Deckers rose a total of 2900% over 4 years. With that said, you would have needed to invest less than 2 years to turn a 660% profit ($5 - $38). And in this case, you would have been out of this market long before distribution even began.

(Chart courtesy of Prophet.Net)

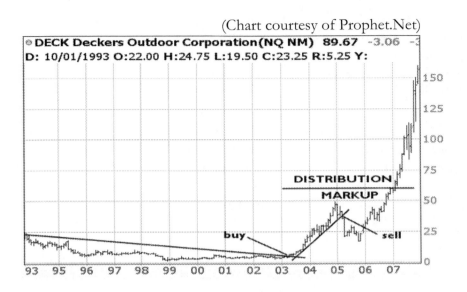

Let's have a look at the chart for McDermott International . This chart reveals that your only and best decision would have been to sell on the break of the trend line at about $23 in 2006. The fact that the price action was becoming choppy, the trend line was almost vertical, and prices had already risen 525% ($5 - $48) would have been enough of a signal to get out. This would have netted you a profit of 475% in 2 years.

(Chart courtesy of Prophet.Net)

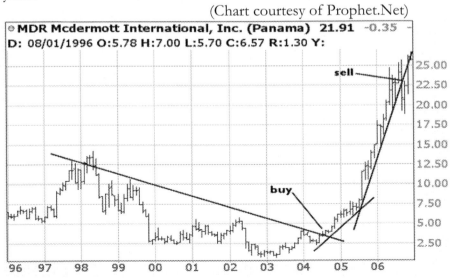

However, what looked like distribution during 2005 and 2006, in fact, turned out to be part of the markup phase as evidenced by the following chart for McDermott. We can see that prices didn't even really start to take off until they broke above $27.50. The resulting steep climb to $62.50 expanded the charts vertical axis which in turn compressed the price action preceding it, turning what originally appeared to be distribution into a more modestly sloping trend line during markup. Since we couldn't see this price action in advance though, the best we could have done at the time was to react to what we did see in 2005 and 2006 and sell when given the signal. Again, we don't need to stay invested from the very bottom to the very top in order to make incredible profits. In this case we would have been invested for less than half of the total rise but still turned a 475% profit – not bad.

(Chart courtesy of Prophet.Net)

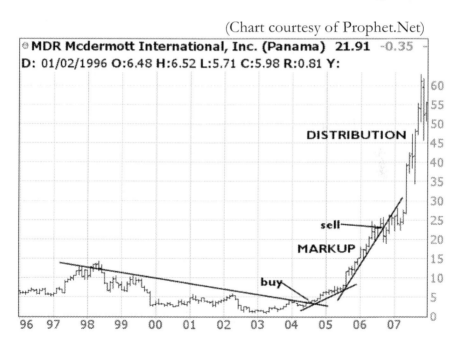

Laboratory Corp is another example of how often you will find yourself out of a stock well before it ever reaches its peak. But that's OK. Had you bought on the breakout of the base in 2000 and then sold on the break of the steep uptrend line at about $35 in 2001, you would have still managed a 250% profit in less than a year. Sometimes the price action will appear distribution-like as it did here from 2000 – 2002 and cause you to sell. Other times the markup will be slow and steady with no major setbacks, allowing you to hang on for more of a ride. The best we can do is to take what each is willing to offer and move on to the next one. And, there is always a next one.

(Chart courtesy of Prophet.Net)

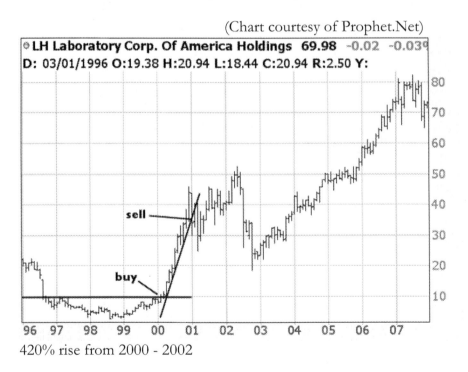

420% rise from 2000 - 2002

Pason System Inc. is an example of a markup phase where you may have been able to hold on for a little longer. After the uptrend line was established by rising prices during 2003 and 2004, the price action that followed in 2005 did setback but only as far as our trend line, where it was then supported before continuing higher. In this case you would have been holding on into distribution and then sold when the third and steepest trend line was broken at about $15.50 in 2006. This would have resulted in a 416% profit ($3.00 - $15.50) in less than 3 years.

(Chart courtesy of Prophet.Net)

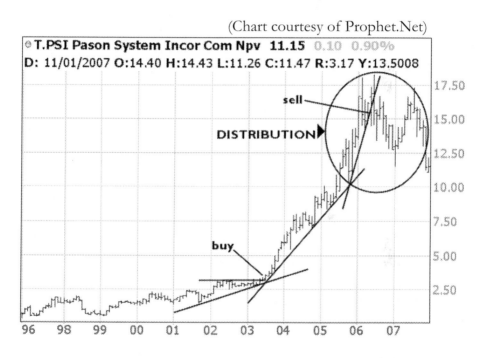

Unlike some stocks which spend as much as 10 years in distribution like MGIC Invest Corp. (page 156), Dialysis Corp. finished its distribution phase in only 9 months and then quickly moved on to markdown. In this case, prices rose so quickly that the trend line literally became vertical.

(Chart courtesy of Prophet.Net)

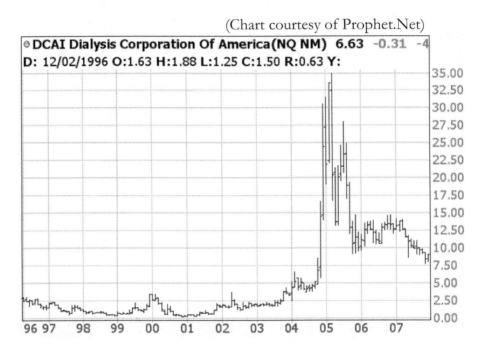

In order to follow this one up, you would have had to change your field of view to a shorter time frame (i.e. a one year chart). This would have allowed you to establish your trend lines and also to be on the lookout for a selling opportunity because you know that when prices rise this quickly they will just as likely fall at the same speed. As it turns out, you would have probably be shaken free on the major setback during Dec. 2004 (see next page) but you would have been rewarded with a 250% profit in only 10 weeks.

Stocks like Dialysis Corp. are the reason we diversify - in the hope that we can catch some of these quicker markups, knowing that we'll surely get stuck holding some of the longer, slower ones.

(Chart courtesy of Prophet.Net)

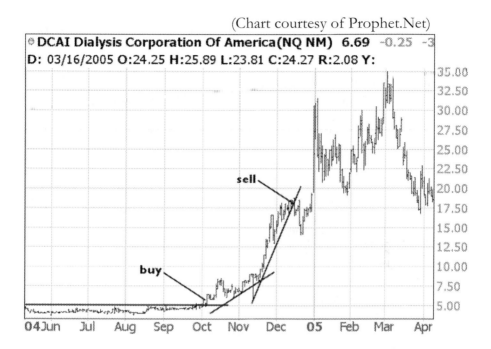

As the trend lines became steeper and steeper during markup you knew that either a sharp setback or distribution was right around the corner. As such, your job at the time was to be watchful and be on the lookout for a selling opportunity.

Regardless of the type of investment, greed comes from a need for speed, but usually results in your misdeed (or losses), whereas patience, backed with faith, results in mastery.

You need to separate yourself from the common perception that stocks are fast but risky while mutual funds are slow but safe. If you sow seeds based on your knowledge, practice and understanding of the man-made price cycle, then success must be your harvest.

Note that during 1998 and 1999 when most of the big name, big-cap stocks were making their ways to all time highs, Hirsch International was on its way from $26 to $1.00. Do you see how each individual stock follows the beat of its own drummer? It doesn't matter what is happening with the rest of the market, prices move based on what the Manipulators need to accomplish at the time. In this case, they had finished selling their shares to the public and by the beginning of 1998 (with no Manipulators left to support prices) markdown gathered steam and speed.

(Chart courtesy of Prophet.Net)

STOCK MARKET MYTH # 8
If you want better returns, you must be willing to take on more risk

Securities experts rank investment vehicles according to risk.

High Risk

Low Risk

Commodities

Common Stock

Mutual Funds

Preferred Shares

Debentures

Bonds

GIC's

Perception tells us that this makes sense, surely commodities are more risky than stocks which are more risky than mutual funds which are more risky than GIC's. But, as we know, perception is not always reality, as here is yet another example.

Risk itself is not attached to any particular investment vehicle. Risk or lack of it comes from each individual's knowledge and ability at investing in the vehicle of their choice. Think about this.

Risk is defined as exposing oneself to a loss. Millions of people every year invest in GIC's at a rate of return that is actually lower than the current rate of inflation and taxes. In this case, not only are these people exposing themselves to a loss, they are guaranteeing it. And after all, isn't the whole point of investing to make money - to end up with more than when you started.

So I ask you, what's riskier, someone who has no knowledge of investing and no desire to learn and sinks all of their money into GIC's for a guaranteed loss on their money every year, or someone with a high level of knowledge and years of practical experience, who invests in, and turns a profit every year in stocks?

What's more risky, someone who has a very clear understanding of the man-made price cycle and how to apply the principles in order to produce positive returns every year in commodities or, someone who has no knowledge of investing in stocks but is determined to day trade based on tips from friends and input from the media because everybody else is doing it?

It's not the investment vehicle that brings the risk. It is very clearly the investors themselves. The riskiest thing any of us can do is to become complacent in our education and our practice. The **risk resides within you** so when you hear someone talking about risk or when you yourself are thinking about risk as it relates to your portfolio say to yourself, "it's up to me to take the risk out of the equation by learning and studying and gaining more knowledge". That is what this book is all about - gaining knowledge and experience by way of study and practice. This, more than anything, will help you to reduce your risk, regardless of your investment vehicle of choice.

There is only one way to lose money in the stock market after all (to sell at a lower price than where you bought in, not including short selling). So, if you've ever lost money on a stock, or many stocks, as I'm sure most of us have, then we must all ask ourselves, am I going to let this keep happening over and over again? I say NO. This is why I wrote this book, to turn the tables on the Manipulators and make it an even playing field again.

You must learn to go against your natural inclinations, your natural urges. What seems right is not right. Is it so hard to believe that with multi-millions of dollars at stake, people, who have the knowledge and the resources to pull this off, wouldn't? Of course they would. Greed, want, and selfishness are powerful motivators. They say to themselves, if the faceless masses of the public must bear the burden so that we may succeed and profit, then so be it. Someone has to lose in a stock transaction and you can bet your socks that it isn't going to be them.

STOCK MARKET MYTH #9
You Can't Time the Market

Who wants to? We don't need to be able to time "THE MARKET".
We're not investing our money in "THE MARKET" (the Dow Jones
or the NASDAQ), we're investing in individual stocks, each of which
is involved in its own price cycle. Having read to this point and seen
example after example after example, I'm sure you have a new
appreciation for and a new perception about timing. You will find that
with lots of practice, you will be able to develop an incredible ability to
accurately time your entry and exit points to maximize profits - just so
long as you do it with a price cycle perspective.

Timing is not about today or tomorrow, it's about when markup
begins and then when distribution-like price action begins. That is all
the timing you need concern yourself with. Timing could mean getting
in and out of a stock within weeks or it could mean buying and holding
for 10 years. It all depends on how long the markup phase lasts for
each particular stock that you invest in. Timing is dictated by the price
cycle - not by you, not when you happen to have extra cash handy for
investing, and certainly not when the experts recommend you buy.

Timing with a price cycle perspective is buying on the breakout of
a large formation after a multi-year accumulation, and selling when, (i)
prices become violent and choppy during markup or the early stages of
distribution and, (ii) after prices have risen hundreds of percent above
their base. Our ultimate goal is to be invested primarily during the
markup phase. Sometimes we'll enter at the end of an accumulation
phase and other times get out during distribution, but the majority of
our holding time will be during markup. You may have a few other
buy and sell opportunities or signals along the way up, but, this is the
big picture as it relates to the man-made price cycle and this is the way
you will routinely maximize your opportunities.

Your goal is to be invested primarily during the markup phase
when prices are rising off the bottom. This is when higher prices are
inevitable as a result of Manipulator control and this is when you have

a cushion of profits to help back up your faith each time prices stall or setback. Holding on too long during distribution can be a risky endeavor. As you have seen, markdown can begin rather suddenly at times, and can be quite severe in its fall. With that in mind, it is best not to be invested too far along into the distribution phase as you never know exactly when prices will begin their descent.

Having a price cycle perspective is your best chance at success in the equity markets. And, is the only way to consistently buy low and sell high.

One thing is for sure, if you keep doing what you're doing, you're going to get more of what you've got. And, if what you've got so far are mostly losses, then you had better change what you are doing.

Short Selling

This is a technique whereby you sell shares first and then buy them back later to close out your position. If you short a stock, prices fall, and then you buy them back later at a lower price, you make money. If you short a stock, prices rise, and then you buy them back at a higher price, you lose money. It is the exact opposite of buying low and selling high to turn profits.

Short selling can be a very effective way to make a lot of money in a short time because as you have seen, more often than not, prices tend to fall faster than they rise. But with that reward comes much risk – too much risk as far as I'm concerned. Why, because of WHERE you enter the market. If you want to make money short selling, then you want to enter at as high a price as possible because you make money when prices go down. The only problem is, this means you would be entering the market during the wild, choppy, volatile distribution phase of the price cycle. And, as you have seen, it is a very difficult task to pick the ultimate top. During distribution there are usually multiple tops with prices falling and rising very quickly. If you choose wrong, prices can go against you in a hurry.

Distribution does not provide the same kind of easy to recognize and accurate entry signals that you get when buying on the breakout of an accumulation base or a consolidation period during early markup. During accumulation and early markup it is easy to identify when a false ceiling sets up over the course of many months or years and just as easy to enter on the breakout of that false ceiling. Distribution is the exact opposite. It is very violent, by no means sideways, and takes place in a relatively short period of time compared to that of its base. Therefore, it presents a much more difficult task at choosing an entry point. Remember the point of distribution is to persuade the public to buy in the top range by the use of encouraging price action. What that translates into on your price chart is not only fast swings in price, but usually higher highs as well.

With all that you have seen and learned there is no reason to sell short because there are just too many opportunities to garner significant profits by buying in at the bottom. When it comes to the price cycle, risk is associated with the upper stages of markup, distribution and, of course, markdown. You can remove almost all of that risk by buying low and selling higher, therefore why would you choose to short?

There are only two reasons to sell short, (1) if you believe what the experts and media tell you about being immersed in a BEAR market and that you'll have a very hard time making any money or, (2) if you're greedy and the markup phase of the stocks you have selected are not making their ways to new highs fast enough for your liking.

However, based on what you have learned in this book, you now know that there is no such thing as a BEAR market and that there are always opportunities to find stocks transitioning from accumulation to markup, always opportunities to buy low and sell high regardless of what other more well known stocks are doing at the time. So, you can't use that as an excuse to sell short. That leaves you with greed, and greed usually means speed. You want it and you want it fast. Just be aware that should you choose to sell short, then with each opportunity to make some fast money comes an equally scary opportunity to lose it, just as quickly.

If distribution can be likened to us finally reaching our treasure chest, opening it, and reaping our rewards, then the markdown phase signifies a realization that we have emptied the treasure chest, and it's time to move onto our next opportunity, our next treasure map.

To stay with the current opportunity or to jump back in after reaping your rewards in the top range would be the same as hanging around an empty treasure chest waiting for the pirates to return to take back their treasure. And, when they return, if the treasure chest is empty and you're still hanging around, then they are going to take it back from you. That's the **markdown** phase and that's what's in store for you if you don't make tracks in the other direction.

Markdown Phase

How do the Manipulators do it? It's one thing to trick the public into buying when prices are racing to all time highs, but it's quite another feat entirely to be able to get the public to buy as prices are falling. In many cases, the Manipulators are not 100% sold out of their position when distribution ends, therefore, their involvement continues on into markdown.

Their #1 weapon during markdown is more of an indirect by-product of the public's greed turned to hope. Investors who bought at the top out of greed find themselves quickly holding losses and clinging to a new found "HOPE" that prices will somehow rebound in their favour. That any setback they are experiencing will be merely temporary. Little do they know that they are the victims left holding the bag. The Manipulators having just unloaded on them in the top range are no longer around to help support prices, at least not the way they did during markup. Without that coordinated effort that only the Manipulators can manage, prices become very heavy and teeter on the edge of a great cliff. And, once they gain momentum and start to roll over that edge, the result is usually a dramatic fall. It is inevitable. Markdown follows distribution as surely as distribution follows markup. It is the pre-meditated cycle of events that takes place for all stocks. It is the man-made price cycle.

Markdown is characterized by prices which fall consistently to new lows after distribution. What happens when the Manipulators have finished selling their millions of shares to the public in the top range? Prices become very unstable.

Imagine a dinner plate sitting on top of a pillar that is 12" in diameter. This would be a very stable structure. The plate would be well supported and have very little chance of falling. We can liken the pillar in our example to that of the Manipulators still holding and owning the majority of their shares. But now imagine taking away the pillar and replacing it with 100 pencils. Let's liken the pencils in our example to that of the public now owning the majority of the shares. This would certainly be a much less stable support system.

Now imagine that 100 people each grab hold of one of the pencils and altogether they attempt to raise the plate in the air. What would happen? The plate would fall of course. Not because they didn't all have the same goal, but because their effort was uncoordinated. Some would apply more pressure while others would apply less pressure and each person would apply their pressure a little faster or a little slower than the person beside them. The result would be a very unstable support with the plate falling and crashing to the floor.

(Chart courtesy of Prophet.Net)

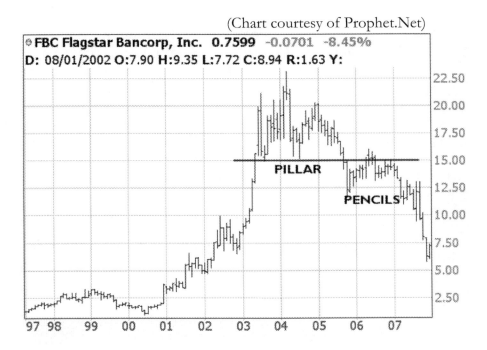

During markup and into the early stages of distribution, the Manipulators still hold the majority of their stock before they unload it onto the public, thus exhibiting a solid, unified, coordinated support system. Remember what they have gone through to this point. They kept prices low for maybe 3 - 5 years or more in order to accumulate a large position in the bottom range. Then they proceeded to sneak prices higher and higher during the markup phase, which perhaps lasted another 3 or 5 or 8 years. So to this point, they may have invested up to 10 - 15 years of their time and millions of dollars of their resources. And, they have brought prices all the way up, perhaps

500% - 2000% higher than where they purchased their shares initially. Is there any doubt that they will not support prices up here at the top end until they are able to sell off their holdings? Any selling pressure can be quickly absorbed because they have huge bank accounts to back them up. All they have to do is overload the bid side of the order desk with buy orders and the public will feel that prices are strong and well supported - as they were for Flagstar Bancorp (previous page) during 2003, 2004 and part of 2005.

But, as more and more of the Manipulator's shares are sold, two things happen simultaneously.

1. The Manipulator's position decreases in size,
2. and the public's position increases in size.

This causes there to be less and less support for prices up in the top range. The once strong coordinated effort that got prices this high in the first place and then kept them up diminishes week by week, month by month, year by year. More and more public shareholders provide less and less support for prices as the public gains a larger and larger percentage of the outstanding shares. We move from pillar to pencils and the more of the public that gets involved in buying, the more pencils we have trying to support our fragile plate.

When the vast majority of the Manipulators are sold out, the structure has evolved to its most unstable stage and the first little bit of pressure will cause a cascading effect that the public will not be able to stop even though they all have the same goal of higher prices. Prices will start to fall. The public who are not in will stay out, and the public who are shareholders will start to get nervous, waiting and hoping for someone else to step in and buy to support prices. But, of course we all know what happens. The investing public being a fickle bunch, start to lose faith more quickly than those who are optimistic and buying. The selling pressure increases and prices gain momentum as they fall.

If somehow, all of the public shareholders were able to communicate with each other, and all get on the same page and decide not to sell, they would in effect duplicate what the Manipulators had done before them and prices would be supported. However, we know this will never happen and as each shareholder puts a different and varying amount of pressure on their pencil, the plate starts to wobble and pretty soon it falls. As prices drop lower and lower and as the drop increases in speed, it is just a matter of time before the plate crashes and breaks.

(Chart courtesy of Prophet.Net)

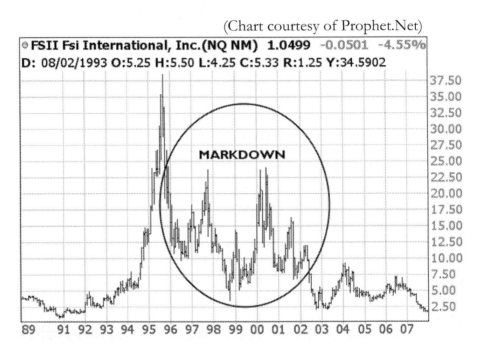

Sometimes markdown is extremely fast, other times prices just seem to slowly drift downwards month after month, year after year, searching for a bottom. In either case, the exact same thing is happening. Investors who were tricked into buying at the top, are now bearing the burden of an uncoordinated effort. Each little rally gives them cause to hold on in hopes that prices will make their way back up to levels were they entered the market. But each temporary rally is just that, temporary, and prices continue their downward spiral. As they do, the stress and frustration levels rise and each investor is now left to find relief in their own way and at their own time. Some will sell after prices have dropped 10%. Others will wait until prices have fallen 50%, and still others won't sell until prices have fallen 90%.

And who are these last "hangers-on" selling to? The Manipulators. Why? Because prices are a bargain again. The Manipulators are ready to start accumulating another position for themselves in the bottom range.

(Chart courtesy of Prophet.Net)

This markdown phase for Tenet Healthcare, although extreme, is not as uncommon as you may think. Sometimes distribution will take the form of one sharp peak prior to markdown. The Manipulators of Tenet were obviously able to sell off all of their shares on the way up to the top. With that, the majority of shares were transferred to the public's weak hands. And, whenever that is the case, prices become very unstable because unlike the Manipulators who have both the resources and the coordinated effort to control and support prices, the public does not.

With that said though, you as a Manipulator savvy investor would have easily recognized when to walk away with your profits. Had you been in this market you would have expected a sharp drop after having watched prices rise as quickly as they did. You may not have known what form the inevitable drop-off would take, but that wouldn't matter. You were given a clear signal when the steep trend line was broken at approx. $45 in 2002. This is a situation where you would have sold quite close to markdown, however, this is usually not the case. Most often, distribution will churn in the top range for years resulting in one higher high after another. In these cases you will have sold out long before markdown ever gets underway. Here's a perfect example.

(Chart courtesy of Prophet.Net)

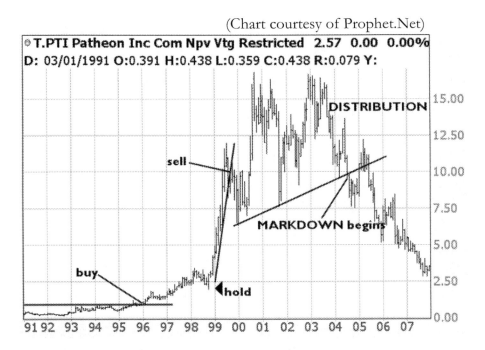

As you can see, the markdown phase for Patheon didn't get under way until 2004. By this time you would have been out of this market for 5 years having sold back in 1999 (well before the peak was ever reached). This will most often be the case, especially for stocks that have large accumulation bases behind them. Why? Because large bases translate into extremely large positions for the Manipulators, and the larger their position the longer, in most cases, it will take for them to unload it. Hence, the picture that results on your long term chart will be one of several years worth of violent and very active price action in the top range.

Just as you received a very clear sell signal in 1999, the beginning of the markdown phase offered up a very clear signal itself when the 5 year uptrend line (defining the lower limits of the distribution phase) was broken.

(Chart courtesy of Prophet.Net)

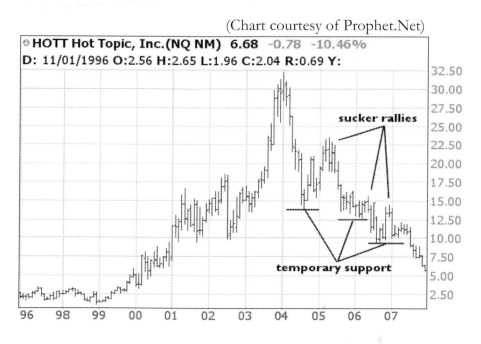

Notice how the markdown phase for Hot Topic experienced periods of temporary support during its fall. When prices first made their way down to $13.50 in 2004, they quickly rebounded back above $22.50 giving hope to anyone who had bought in higher or offering short term opportunities to speedy speculators who thought prices were now a bargain compared to their previous $32.50 highs. These are merely sucker rallies during a falling market and as a student of the price cycle they are easy to avoid because they are easy to see.

But again, as most investors are not aware of the big picture and do not consult long term charts for their investing strategy, they are simply left with news reports and the recommendations of others to guide them. No matter what the news or fundamentals, there is no reason to invest in a falling market when there are so many other opportunities in the bottom range.

Hot Topic won't be a consideration for quite some time now. Prices are still making new lows and even after they do reach their final bottom they will then need to accumulate for some time prior to another significant rise. Therefore, when the price picture looks like it does here, simply hit your skip button and move onto the next one.

(Chart courtesy of Prophet.Net)

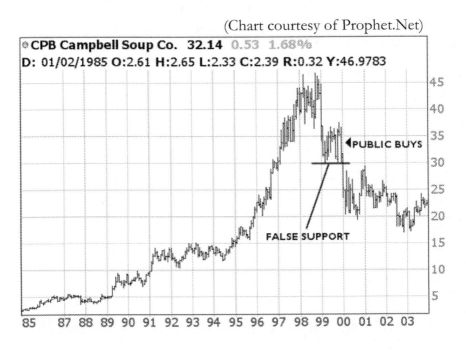

This picture of Campbell Soup reveals much. First and foremost that it is currently involved in markdown, and therefore, we should stay away. Again, notice the temporary level of support that occurred during markdown. These levels have the same effect as false ceilings during markup, except are opposite in nature. False ceilings during markup give the impression that prices are weak and unable to go higher, therefore, the public sells or stays away. But prices do continue to rise. False support levels during markdown give the impression that prices are strong and will likely not go lower, therefore, the public buys or at least holds hoping for a recovery rally. But, of course, prices continue to fall.

Prices for Campbell Soup had trouble falling below $30 for all of 1999 giving the public the "impression" that they were well supported and strong and, therefore, would likely rise from this level. Of course we know that this kind of price action in most cases means the exact opposite, and this is why we refer to these levels as FALSE support. With some remaining shares to dispose of, the Manipulators know that the only way they will get the public to buy from them, is to make prices appear strong and encouraging. So, that's what they do. Or should I say that's what they do "temporarily". The public buys from $30 to $37, the Manipulators sell and again the public is left holding the bag when prices finally continue their fall.

The public thought they were getting a real bargain at $30, after all, prices for Campbell Soup had just been as high as $47. And, since the media and analysts were still singing their praises, why not buy? The entire market was rocketing straight up to one new high after another during 1999. The DOW and NASDAQ could do no wrong. You couldn't talk to a friend, read a paper, or watch the news, without hearing about how well the stock market was doing. Everyone thought they could make some quick easy money. Of course, as Manipulator savvy investors you now know that "THE MARKET" doesn't matter. The only thing that matters is the price cycle of each individual stock.

(Chart courtesy of Prophet.Net)

What was happening with Unisys Corp. (previous page) from 2004 to 2005 as prices were falling from $170 down to $50? All those investors who had bought in the $100 - $170 range during the previous year, (because they thought prices had hit bottom), were now selling back to the Manipulators at lower prices. The Manipulators wore them down over time causing them to sell lower after having bought higher, and the entire man-made price cycle begins again.

Remember, the price cycle is a continuous unending process. As one phase completes, another begins, as one cycle completes, another begins. This simply means that accumulation follows markdown just as markdown follows distribution. As prices approached the bottom, the public was selling out at lower prices for fear of bigger losses and the Manipulators were only too happy to snatch up a bargain.

Even though Unisys is back in the bottom range again, it's still not a buy, why? Because prices have to accumulate again prior to their next significant rise. Buying back in too early means tying up your money and watching it go sideways, possibly for many years. Now yes, prices could bounce right back up to $100 and you might be able to turn a quick profit. On the other hand, prices could just as easily continue to fall to $10 and then trade sideways for years. Then not only would you be holding losses, but that money wouldn't be available to work for you in other opportunities where prices were actually rising.

In some cases, markdown will end and accumulation will begin before prices fall all the way back down to where they started their original climb. In these situations, the accumulation phase will take place at levels that are much higher than their original base. When this happens, we refer to these accumulations as high-level bases.

(Chart courtesy of Prophet.Net)

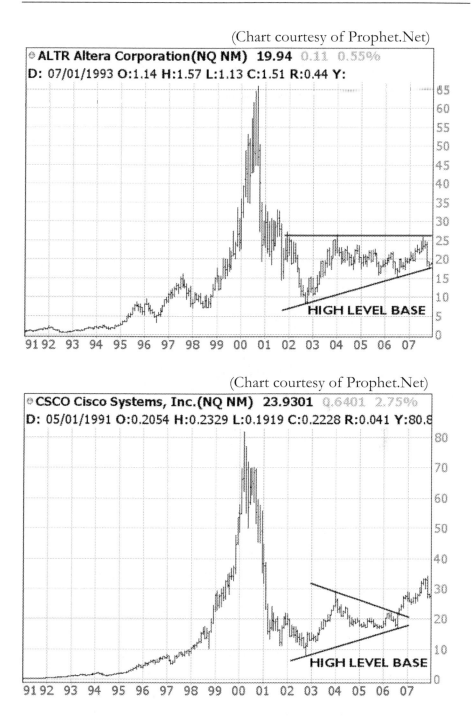

(Chart courtesy of Prophet.Net)

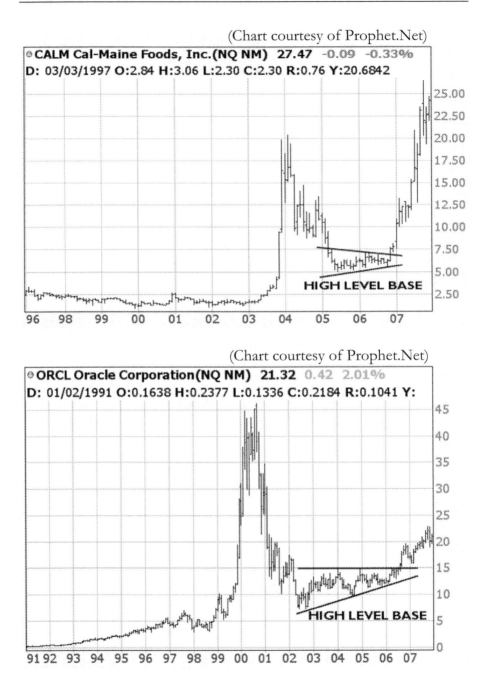

(Chart courtesy of Prophet.Net)

(Chart courtesy of Prophet.Net)

Oracle shows us the perfect example of a high-level base. For four and a half years prices set up a flat-top triangle with a false ceiling at $15. The more time that is spent in this triangle the better, just as with all formations. However, you still have to ask yourself if buying on the break of this triangle is the best use of your money, with the least amount of risk, for the best potential return, in the shortest period of time. When considering all these factors, one would have to conclude, NO.

Let's run through the reasoning one point at a time.

1. Buying on the break of a high-level base will always have a higher risk factor than buying a stock at the bottom simply because prices have more room to fall. As well, what might seem like a high level base could turn out to be a false support level during the markdown phase. Remember there are no absolutes when it comes to investing in stocks.

2. Buying a stock on the breakout of a high-level base means buying in at a much higher price than if you were to buy down at the bottom (on the breakout of an accumulation base). As a result, your chance of earning the greatest percentage return will always be with a buy at the bottom. For example, the rise for Cal-Maine Foods (previous page) from $2.50 - $20 in 2003 represents a 700% rise whereas the move from $7.50 to $27 in 2007 represents only a 260% rise even though prices advanced further during this second move. Because of its higher breakout point, Cal-Maine would have to reach $60 now to produce the same 700% rise that occurred in 2003.

3. Using the same example, the time taken for Cal-Maine to move from $2.50 to $20 to produce a 700% return would not necessarily be any faster or slower than buying this stock on the breakout of its high-level base at $7.50 and waiting for it to reach $60. Therefore, the time to profit is also not a persuading factor to buy on the breakout of the high-level base.

Therefore, one would have to conclude from this that the best use of your money will be to buy sound stocks on the breakout of long, quiet accumulation bases in the bottom range.

Summary

The most concise way for me to summarize everything that you have read so far, (keeping in mind that this is a "how to" book and the main purpose is to provide you with practical tools that you can immediately employ to your benefit), would be to say:

"Buy sound stocks in the bottom range, but only after the breakout of a multi-year accumulation base, and/or consolidation periods during early markup and then be patient and sell when both of the following criteria have been met; the breaking of a steep uptrend line in conjunction with a large percentage rise off the base."

That's it in a nutshell. But to make this possible, it is up to you to practice and practice in order to gain the faith to follow through. Faith is not acquired overnight. It is not acquired through a book or from another person. It is only internalized and accepted over time, through your own efforts to take action. This action is to view and study one long range chart after another until you have seen so many price cycles that your eyes go bleary. The more you accept and believe in the man-made price cycle, the more you will trust and take action on it - and, the more successful you will be. Remember, everything that you need to know to make an informed investment decision is right there in front of you on the long term chart.

Beware of fundamentals; beware of the media; beware of the so-called experts. Don't let them narrow your field of view. There is no such thing as a BEAR market as it applies to you. The media and market experts will tell you that it is very difficult to make money during their "so called" BEAR markets. But that simply is not the case. Anyone who tells you this is coming at you from one of two positions.

1. They either don't know about the man-made price cycle, which makes taking their advice a questionable endeavor or,

2. they are aware of the man made price cycle but are purposefully trying to mislead you.

In either case, relying on yourself, for your own investment decisions will be your safest and most successful path to financial success.

Some of you may have counted, but for those who haven't, I have done it for you. Throughout this book, I have presented 60 different stocks, all of which have risen anywhere from 20% - 4600% during their so-called BEAR market (2000-2003). And these are just some of the stocks that have made these kind of moves. There are hundreds more. It seems to me that this should be proof enough of the fact that stocks do not trade based on what the "market" is doing but rather based on what their own individual price cycle dictates.

Awareness on its own will go a long way towards allowing you to control your emotions, but practice will lead to a greater understanding and a greater faith. Emotions will always be present when your hard earned money is at stake, but no longer will the media, experts and analysts be able to excite or frighten you with their "words of wisdom", causing you to second guess your investment plans. You have a big picture perspective now. You know that there is a conscious effort on the part of some to deceive, so you'll be ready for their tricks.

And, not only will you NOT be taken in by them, but you will now be able to take advantage of the fact that all stocks move in the same repeatable, predictable fashion.

WHY? Because all stocks are the same.

ADDENDUM

Why I Went to Cash in January, 2008

As with most people, a fair percentage of my total portfolio is made up of mutual funds and ETF's. And as you know, each fund is simply a collection of many stocks. Unfortunately, it is not easy (even for a Manipulator savvy investor) to look at the individual price cycle for perhaps the top 20 – 30 stocks in each particular fund and then determine how each will influence the fund's overall performance. So, how does one then determine how their funds will perform?

What is important to recognize is that most fund managers invest in only the largest cap stocks, those very same stocks which usually comprise the major North American & International stock indices. Therefore, most funds' price action will move in sync with the index that they are representing (i.e. a US Technology Fund will track almost exactly the same as the NASDAQ index; a China Fund will track almost exactly the same as the Shanghai Composite; a Canadian Large Cap Fund will track almost exactly the same as the S&P TSX). So, in this case, and this case only, the indices do give us an indication of how many of the most popular mutual funds/ETF's are performing and will likely perform in the future.

Because of this intertwined relationship, I follow not only each individual fund's long term price chart but also the major North American and International indices as well. So, when I noticed the steep run up of all of the North American indices at the same time between 2003 – 2007, I knew that a violation of that uptrend line would signal a major market reversal just as it did in 2000 and 1987 and 1973, et al. And in turn, all of the funds that tracked those same indices would follow in lock step

At the same time (to provide further confirmation) I was following each individual fund's long term chart, as well as the top 10 holdings (stocks) within each fund. All price charts were providing the same information (steeply rising prices in the top range).

And, just as with individual stocks, when steep uptrend lines are violated after years of significant gains, it's time to look for a sell signal – and that sell signal came in January, 2008.

(Chart courtesy of Prophet.Net)

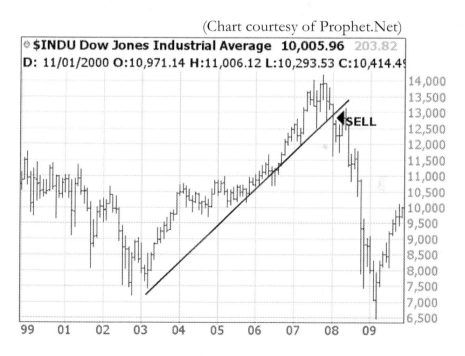

Just as SELL is investing's "four letter" word, so too is "CASH". Again, the media and experts have brainwashed us into believing that holding cash is bad. That holding cash is no way to accumulate wealth. Well, sometimes CASH is KING. Cash is merely a by-product of selling. In order to raise cash someone must first sell some of their investments. But since fundamentalists are terrified to sell because their data doesn't give them any signals about when to enter or exit markets, they are trapped forever in the world of buy and hold. Or should I say the world of buy, and then sit and wait for their stocks/funds to recover from their most recent 40 – 50% crash.

In retrospect, I'm sure most would agree that a 1% – 2% positive return of interest on your cash is a lot more appealing than a 40 – 50% plunge of your total portfolio. We don't live forever, therefore, we need to maximize our time invested. For those of you who have been invested in the markets these past 10 years and just watched as your portfolio rose in the 90's and then plunged in 2000 and then finally recovered by 2007 only to fall off another cliff in 2008, it's time to realize that SELL and CASH are not bad words. They are simply tools to a more profitable investment approach which will allow you to protect your capital during times of extreme downturns. And, now that you are aware of why prices move the way they do, buying back in near the bottom is not the "mystical endeavor" that the so-called experts would have you believe it is.

Holding cash applies equally to individual stocks as well. Most of us have full time jobs and only have time to work on our investments during our spare time. And in that limited spare time that we do have, we can only follow so many charts. But what if the charts that you have searched through don't offer up any buy signals? There may be tens or even hundreds of stocks offering up buy signals at any particular time as they break out of accumulation bases and/or consolidation periods during early markup. But if you aren't aware of them, if you haven't uncovered them yet – then your job is to keep looking – NOT to invest for the sake of being invested. You don't want to put your money into stocks that are midway through accumulation, or on into distribution or worse yet, those in markdown just because you can't find those offering up appropriate buy signals. Hold cash, be patient and keep searching, because there are always stocks in markup. Your job is to find them.

Index of Stock Charts